How to Unlock Windows Speech Recognition

Other Books by Larry C Carlson

~How to Self-Publish for Under $10.00~

Editor - Living Free Handbook~

How to Unlock Windows Speech Recognition And Other Free Applications

Larry C Carlson

ElCar Publishing, LLC

Wausau WI

Copyright © 2020 Larry C Carlson

Please respect, the Author and the law and do not participate in or encourage piracy of copyrighted materials. All rights reserved. No part of this book may be reproduced or transmitted in any form without written permission from the Author, except in the manner of brief quotations embodied in critical articles and reviews. Every effort has been made to be accurate. The Author assumes no responsibility or liability for errors made in this book.

Trademarks: Windows, Word, Windows Speech Recognition, Vista, Windows 7, Windows 8, Windows 8.1, Windows 10, Surface, WordPad, Notepad, and all other products, applications, or accessories of the Microsoft Corporation are trademarks of Microsoft Corporation; CreateSpace and Kindle Direct Publishing are registered trademarks of Amazon.com, Inc. Lulu is a registered trademark of Lulu Press, Inc. All other trademarks are property of their respective owners.

Except for their own books, ElCar Publishing LLC is not associated with any company, product or vendor mentioned in this book.

ISBN: 9781657765351

Cover Design by the Author

TABLE OF CONTENTS

INTRODUCTION

TYPING ON PC A PROBLEM?

Why This Book 1
Microsoft Windows Speech
Recognition 1
What is Speech Recognition 2
Wikipedia 2
WHAT? 2
Is it a Secret? 3
Questions? 3
Word Processing 4
Require Microsoft Word? 4
WordPad OpenOffice LibreOffice 4
Other Questions 5
Why People Are Not Using 6
Experience with WSR 6
On Its Own Merits - TopTenReview 7
Compare to Commercial Programs 8
We Take This Test 8
Appendix – The Test 8
aNewDomain 9
Our Test Results 9
Our Goal 10
An Alternative 10
Editing Capabilities 11
Learning Writing Skills 11

~CHAPTER ONE~
The First Key-Microsoft Windows

The first key Free Application 13
Windows Speech Recognition 13
First Step - Stop Typing! What? 13
Do Not Be Misled 14

COMPATIBLE MICROSOFT APPLICATIONS

Microsoft OneNote 15
Sticky Notes 16
Word Pad/ Windows 7 16
WordPad/ Vista 16
Setting Up Word Editor /Processor 17
No Special Format For Now 17

~CHAPTER TWO~
How it Works
A Non-Technical View

Simplified Illustration of Process 19
Not "Sleight of Hand" 20
Not Easy but Easier 20-21

THREE ESSENTIAL REQUIREMENTS

Compatible Word Processor 22
Compatible Microphone 22
Desk Top Microphones 22
Speak Clearly 23

~CHAPTER THREE~
Introduction to
Microsoft Speech Recognition
Ok – It's all New

The Concept – This is a Tutorial 25
Application vs. Program 26
Speech Recognition is Speech-to-Text
Conversion 26
Editing a Significant Advantage 26
Not Voice Recognition 27
Not Automatic 27
[Commands] 27
Preview Commands - Alternatives 28
[Commands] (Subcommands) 28
Preview Examples 28

MAXIMIZE LEARNING

Learn from Incorrect Responses 29
Best and Worst Practices 30
The Unexpected [Save] 30
Enable Dictation Scratchpad 31
Improving Word Selection 32

~CHAPTER FOUR~
Microsoft Windows Speech Recognition
Set Up Procedure

Vista and Windows 7 33
Windows 8 33
Windows 10 33

SETUP PROCEDURE SIMPLIFIED

Begin with Control Panel 34
Speech Properties Window 34
Start or open in off position 35
Create User Name 35
Add User's Profile 35
Take Speech Tutorial 35
Train Your Computer to Better Understand You 35
User's Settings 36
Setting Microphone 36
Microphone Levels 36
Microphone Slider 37

~CHAPTER FIVE~
Introduction Windows Speech Recognition
The "Message Board"

Windows Speech Recognition Module (Message Board) 39
Quick Guide Speech Recognition Module 40
Vista and Windows 7 Tutorial 41
Line 5 A Start Speech Tutorial 41
Line 9 A and B 42
Speech Dictionary Options 42
Add a New Word 42
Mini-Macro Generator 43
Prevent Word from Being Used 44
Change Existing Words 44

End Discussion of Message Board

REVIEW OF SOME COMMANDS

What Can I Say 45

How do I do Something 45
Move Speech Recognition 45
Minimize or Maximize? 46
Create Shortcuts and Bookmarks 46
Bookmarks – Internet Browsers 46
Picture Yourself at the Microphone 47
Key Commands 47
For Windows 8 and 10 47

DO NOT SKIP THE MICROSOFT TUTORIALS

~CHAPTER SIX~
Introduction
To
Quick Guide Table 1 Columns A&B
"Look Ma, No Hands"

Speech Recognition and More 49
Microsoft Windows Speech Recognition 50
Review - Experiment 50
Table 1 Columns A and B 50
Start Listening 50
Stop Listening 52
Table 1 Quick Guide 51
What Can I Say? 52
Show Speech Options 52
Open/Start 52
Cortana 53
Example WordPad 53
Menu Items Can Be Collapsed 53
Word Pad Simple Menu Ribbon 53
Microsoft Word 2013 Ribbon 54
Open Word Processor 54
Show Numbers 55
Show Numbers and Mouse Grid 55
New Line and New Paragraph 55
Say Word not Command 55
Say Word not Number 56
Get Number not Word 56
[Press] Name of Key 57
Individual Capital Letters 57
Repeat Character or Letters 58
Duplicate Keys on Keyboard 58
Foreign Language Keyboard Maps 58

FUNDAMENTAL NAVIGATIONAL COMMANDS

Press [Home] and [End] 59
Go UP/Down – Scroll Up/Down 59

SUMMARY

Commands are the Building Blocks 60
Review Introduction 61

~CHAPTER SEVEN~
The "Magic"
Of
Windows Speech Recognition

HOW DO YOU EAT AN ELEPHANT?

How to Eat An Elephant? 61
He One "Bite" at a Time 61
First Bite Overview 62
Commands/Subcommands 62
The "Magic" of WSR 61
Change Metaphor 62
First Bite 62
Too Difficult? Review Table 63
5 Most Important Commands 63
Commands/Subcommands 63
(Word) (Next/Last/Previous) 64
Three Major Commands 64
Second Bite [Delete] 64
Think Delete Key 64
Change Your Mind? 65
Hesitation 66
Example 66
Directional Deleting 66
[Delete That] (Right/Left) 67
Inside a Word 67
WARNING a Reminder 67
Alternates Panel 68
Editing Words 69
Third Bite 68
[Correct] [Correct that] 69
Break It Down 70
To Undo 70
Dictating Difficult Words 70
Adding/Deleting Characters 71

Use NATO Alphabet 71

NATO QUICK GUIDE

NATO/Signs/Symbols 72
Open Speech Dictionary 73
User's Profile - See Appendix 74
Fourth Bite 74
[Select/Select that] 74
Hesitation (Reminder) 75
Fifth Bite 75
[Delete] [Correct] [Select] with (Word) or (Words) 76
Exercise Caution [Delete] 76
[Correct] 77
Select 77
[Go to] (Before/After) 77
Sixth Bite 77
Go to (Next/Last/Previous) (# of Units) 78
[Go to] and [Go] 78

TIME FOR A BREAK
COUNTING

How Do We Count Words 79
Seventh Bite 79
Counting Characters 80
"Just do it." 80
Where is Your Cursor? 80
Calculating Distance 80
Using [Press] [Ctrl] (h) and (f) 81

THE STARTING POINT

Eighth Bite 81
[Go to] (Next/Previous) (#1 of Units) 81
Always From the Cursor 81
[Delete] 82
[Correct] or [Select] 82
More [Go] Additional Commands 83
[Go to] Pinpoint a Location 84
Experiment With [Go] and [Go to] 84
[Select] (Word… Word) 84
Speech Recognition Tutorials 85

~CHAPTER EIGHT~
Where is the Rabbit?

THE RABBIT IS OUT OF THE HAT

FORMATTING

Additional Formatting Necessary 86
Menus in Notepad 86
Menus WordPad/Windows 7 86
Addition of Ribbon 86
Ribbon Quick Access Toolbar 87
Adding to Quick Access Menu 87
Minimizing Ribbon 87
Table 2 Column A & B 88
[File] Page Setup 89
[File] Page Setup Margins 89
[View] Ruler Word Wrap 90
[Home] Paragraphs Line Spacing 90
Paragraph Pilcrow Options 90
[Home] Expand Collapse Ribbon 91
Other Options 91
[Home] (Font) 91
[Text Color] (Font Color) [Highlight] 91
Change Back to Black 92
[Bold] [Italics] [Underline] [Unselect] 92
Caps No Caps Lowercase 92
[Insert] and [Editing] 92
[Copy [Paste] Cut] 93
[Press] [Ctrl] (f) and (h) 93
Setting Page Size for Books 94
ISO Paper Sizes No Help 94
Better Solution - OpenOffice or Libre Office 95
Settings for WordPad 95
Adjusting WordPad 95
OpenOffice and WordPad 96
Making it More Accurate 96

~CHAPTER NINE~
Enable Dictation Scratchpad

Using [Scratchpad] with Excel 97
Prepare Cells Manually 97
Excel 2010 Spreadsheet 98
Making Entries 98
Totaling Columns (Cells) 99
Direct Entry 99
Excel Mobile 99
Example Excel Mobile 99
Practical Application 100
Not Uniform Results 100
Other Applications 101
Searching the Internet 101
Cortana 101
Google Now Search 101

~CHAPTER TEN ~
Macros for Windows Speech Recognition

Definition 103
Complicated –But Worth It 104
Preview of Steps 104
The Task Bar 104
Composite Image 105
Create a Macro 105
Create Two More Macros 106
Summary 106
Emulate Commands 107
Create Emulate Macros 107
Macros Deactivate on Shutdown 108
Advanced Macros 108

~CHAPTER ELEVEN~
Switching and Navigating

Table 1&Table 2 Pages 51 and 88 109
Navigating Within the Computer 109
[Start] 109
[Open] (From Desktop) 110
Open [Control Panel] 110
[Switch] (Application) 110
[Switch to] (Desktop) 110
Pick a Program 111

NAVIGATING THE INTERNET

Bookmarks Bar 112
Show Numbers/Mouse Grid 111

END SPEECH RECOGNITON TUTORIAL

~CHAPTER TWELVE~
Construction Conversion of Tables

TABLES AND PDF APPLICATIONS

A Five-Step Process 113

THE WORD PROCESSOR

Step One Create Table 114
Step Two Enter Text 114
Create/Adjust Cells 114
Enter Text First 114
Adjust Size of Font and Cells 115
Example of Adjustment 115
Step Three 115
Create Separate Title 115
Example Modified Title 116
Title and Table with Border 117
Formatting Cell Borders 117
Step Four 118
Create PDF File 118

PDF APPLICATIONS

PDF File Applications 119
Primo PDF by Nitro 119
PDF-XChange 119
PDF File Viewers 120
Step Five 120
Create Images 120
Use Ultrafilesearch to Find Files 120
Snipping Tool 120
Edit With Image Editor 120

~CHAPTER THIRTEEN~
Using Paint.NET

Down Load Paint.NET 123

IMORTANT NOTE VISTA – WINDOWS 7

OldApps.com 124
Summary of Paint.NET Menu 124
Image Paint.NET Canvas 125
Composite Menu 125
Rectangle Select Tool 126
Resize 126
Editing a Photograph 127
Formatting the Image 128
Inserting Within Text ? 128
Creating Margins 129
Capitalize a Title 129
Capitalizemytitle.com 129
Inserting Images 129
Image Resize – Set DPI 130
Move Image Tool 130
Alternate Tool 130
Inserting into WordPad 131
Placing Image into Another Image 131
To Improve Clarity 132
Sharpen 132
Open Recent 132
Text and Shapes 133
Obtaining and Editing Images 133
Public Domain and CC0 Images 134
Summary 135

~CHAPTER FOURTEEN~
Recapturing Written Documents

OCR 135
(Optical Character Recognition) 135
Wikipedia Definition 135
FreeOCR – Be Careful! 136
Example of Mixed Quality 137
Document Fonts 137
Application 138
Handwriting OCR 139

~CHAPTER FIFTEEN~
Special-Purpose Applications

SCRIVENER – YWRITER 6

Scrivener 139
Tools of Interest to Novelists 140
Scrivener Word Processor 140
Project Management Tool 140
Popular, Inexpensive, But Complex 140
yWriter6 A Free Application 140
Word Processor for Novels 141
yWriter4 141
yWriter4 Works with WSR 142
Visit Websites 142

SUMMARY

Compare and Decide 143

TEXT-TO-SPEECH

Text-to-Speech 143
The Reverse of Speech-to-Text 143
Wikipedia Working Definition 143
Brief History 143
Enter the Modern Era 144
Speech Synthesis SAPI5 Voices 144

TEXT-TO-SPEECH APPLICATIONS

Text-to-Speech TTS Free 145
Windows Speech Recognition
Compatible 145
TypeIt ReadIt 145
Visual Impairment/Reading 145
Disability 145
Designed to Do? 146
Works for Business 146
Application for Young Children 146
Making a Good Product Better 147
Use With Speech Recognition 147
Change Font Size/Speed 147

COMMERCIAL PRODUCTS

Amazon Ivona Reader 148
Better Quality SAPI Voices 148
S2G Speech2Go 148
S2G Works with Microsoft Speech
Recognition 148
Natural Reader 148
Not Speech Recognition Compatible 148
Good Quality Reasonable Price 148

~CHAPTER SIXTEEN~
The Information Age

Still Communicate with
Printed Text? 149

MULTIPURPOSE APPLICATION

Calibre 150
E-book Library Manager 151

PAPERBACK AND E-BOOK PUBLISHING OPTIONS

For The Self-Motivated Author 151
POD Self-Publishing 151
Technology and Self-Publishing 151
Print on Demand (POD) 151
Has Created Inexpensive Publishing 151
ElCar Publishing Guide 152
How to Self Publish for Under $10.00 152
Formatting Guide 152
Not About Improving Writing 152
Not the Ultimate Authority 152
A Practical Guide 152
Be Careful to Avoid Bad Deals 153
Free Tools 153
Microsoft Word 2003 – 2013 153
Kindle Direct Publishing, (KDP) Lulu
and Smashwords 154

CREATE YOUR OWN WEBSITE

Old Procedures Have Changed 155
Easier to Set up a Website 155
Free Setup and Hosting Available 155
Quality Free Providers 155
Weebly.com 155
Our Website 156

~CHAPTER SEVENTEEN~
**Editing, Proofreading
and
Miscellaneous Resources**

SELF-EDITING, REVISION AND PROOFREADING

Editing 159
Proofreading 159
Learning Writing Skills 160
Words From a Professional 160
Improving Your Skills 160
On Writing Well – Zinsser 160
Secret of Good Writing 161
Rewriting 161
Hard Work 162
Encouragement 162
End of Quotes 162
Learn to Track Changes 163

FREE ONLINE APPLICATIONS AND RESOURCES

Speechnotes, SpeechnotesX – Voice Testing, Google Docs 164
Quick and Easy 162
Advantage – No Tutorials 162
Disadvantage – Limited Editing 162
Slickwrite Online 164
Use Internet Explorer 164
Works With Speech Recognition 164
Multiple Evaluation of Documents 165
grammark.org 165

COMMERCIAL EDITORS

Serenity Editor 165
Grammarly 166
ProWriterAid 166

FREE INTERNET RESOURCES

Tech Tools for Writers 167
Paul Beverly 167
Beyond Paper Editing 167
GrammarBook.com 168
Virustotal 169
Chicago Manual of Style 169
WikiHow to do Anything 169
Purdue Online Writing Lab 169
UNC-Chapel Hill Writing Center 170
University North Carolina Libraries 170
UNC Libraries Citing Sources? 170
The Book Designer 171
Pat McNees – Writers and Editors 171

~~APPENDIX~~

ALTERNATE SPEECH RECOGNITION APPS

Speechnotes/Speechloggger 173

Open Google Chrome 173
Speechnotes/Speechlogger 173
Example Speechnotes 174
Google Docs 175

10 TOP3 TEN REVIEWS – SPEECH RECOGNITION TEST

Copy of Test 176

PROFILE BACKUP AND RESTORE

SpProfileMgr.exe 177
Create New User's Profile 177

OPTIMIZATION UTILITIES

Restart Computer Regularly 179
Check Internet for Optimization 179
Already on Your Computer 179
Four Applications 179
Anti Virus Applications 179

QUICK GUIDES

Speech Recognition Module 181
Table 1 Column A and B 182
Table 2 Column A and B 183
NATO Alphabet Signs & Symbols 184
Alternate Commands 185
Alternate Key Commands 186
ElCar Publishing Website 187
Printable Quick Guides 187
Notes 188-191

~INTRODUCTION~

Why this Book?

Many using PCs with Microsoft operating systems from Vista to Windows 10 create documents. Many are not enthusiastic because they lack good keyboarding skills. Because of their creativity, or out of necessity, they continue to use the keyboard but never seem to improve their keyboard skills.

Whether poor typing is due to a lack of physical dexterity, training or motivation; bad habits, or for a few just plain laziness, it creates additional stress and affects productivity.

Not having good typing skills, we realize how detrimental poor typing can be when working on projects. Constant use of the [Backspace key] and [Delete key] is frustrating, inefficient, time-consuming and can all but destroy creativity.

For those who are serious about improving their computer performance, the first step is to be made aware of and start using an application that is already part of these operating systems.

Microsoft Windows Speech Recognition

The primary focus of this tutorial is to introduce users of PCs with these Microsoft operating systems to Microsoft Windows Speech Recognition. It is an application that is part of these systems. Why? First, the ability to use this application to produce text by voice may be the single most important FREE tool any writer can use to overcome keyboard deficiencies, and increase their productivity.

Second, many who will benefit from it are already using a computer with an adequate microphone. Third, they already have access to additional FREE components also part of these operating systems or available as FREE applications on the Internet.

What is Speech Recognition?

Wikipedia defines it as follows: **"Speech Recognition (SR)** is the disciplinary sub-field of computational linguistics that develops methodologies and technologies that enables the recognition and translation of spoken language into text by computers."

WHAT?
Create Text

Technically that may be an accurate definition, but for most of us it is computer jargon and does little to help most of understand what speech recognition is and how it works.

Let's talk concepts. Speech recognition is an application that uses a microphone connected to a computer which converts voice waves into digital data which is added to a word processor or editor and displayed on a computer monitor. In other words rather than using the keyboard and mouse, the user creates documents by composing (dictating) text and creating documents by voice.

Editing Text

Another important aspect of Windows Speech Recognition is that it not only enables the production of text by voice but also permits editing "on the fly." [Commands] permit the user to make immediate corrections to the text by voice, or when editing, to direct to the curser to a place in the document to make corrections or improvements without using the keyboard. This is part of the "magic" of Windows Speech Recognition.

History

Speech recognition originated with Bell Labs researchers in 1952. It has a long history and involves contributions and improvements from many large corporations working together including Google, Microsoft, IBM, Apple, Amazon, Nuance and others.

It did not become commercially feasible until the late 1990s. Initially it was used to handle large volumes of telephone calls. An application developed by Lernout & Hauspie was used with the Windows XP operating system in 2000, but speech recognition did not become part of the Microsoft operating systems until incorporated into the Vista operating system in 2006.

Is Microsoft Windows Speech Recognition a Secret?

No. Windows Speech Recognition has been part of Microsoft operating systems since Vista. Microsoft has not kept this a secret, but they have not actively advertised it either. We hope to change this.

Questions?

The first question is obvious. Why should you consider Windows Speech Recognition? If you have problems typing, but consistently need to produce a volume of written materials, and are using a PC equipped with a Microsoft operating system that already has Windows Speech Recognition, why not become familiar with it, so you can determine if it will help improve your production?

If you have one of these operating systems you already have two, and maybe three of the necessary components on your computer to use speech recognition. First, you have Windows Speech Recognition and secondly, if using Surface 1, Word 2013. If using a standard operating system and do not have a Microsoft Word application after 2002, you still have two word editors, WordPad and Notepad.

Many computers are equipped with suitable microphones. Check you microphone. If it works you have all the components necessary to begin using use Windows Speech Recognition. If not you can purchase a microphone or headset for under $20.00 from Amazon, Ebay or your local electronics store.

Word Processing

Not surprisingly the ideal word processors to use with Windows Speech Recognition are Microsoft Word processors beginning with Microsoft Word 2002 thru Microsoft Office 365. When referring to Microsoft Word we will refer only to those published after 2002 because they will work seamlessly with Microsoft Windows Speech Recognition application.

We also experimented with Microsoft 2002 and Office 365, but most of the writing was done with using speech recognition using Word 2013. Many sections were purposely composed as an experiment using WordPad, Vista to Windows 10 and pasted into the main text.

Does Windows Speech Recognition Require Microsoft Word?

Is a copy of Microsoft Word 2002 through Microsoft Office 365 necessary in order to use Windows Speech Recognition? The answer is NO.

WordPad OpenOffice and LibreOffice

Another little known fact is that WordPad, a word editor, which is also is part of each of these operating systems, except Surface 1 (which has Microsoft Word 2013) works exceptionally well with Windows Speech Recognition. Some might object to this because it does not have "spell check" and has limited formatting options. While true, WordPad does create text by speech recognition in the same way the Microsoft Word processors do.

This book was written not only to introduce Microsoft Windows Speech Recognition but also to enable its use by as many potential writers as possible.

Microsoft Word processors are complete word processors. They have spell check, advanced formatting features including mirror imaging and the ability to create PDF files. The latter two features are helpful, but not necessary in creating documents that can be printed as books.

We researched to find free non-Microsoft word processors comparable to the Microsoft Word processors. We did not find any, but using WordPad to create text we found two free word processors OpenOffice and LibreOffice that satisfy the other requirements and are readily downloaded as FREE word processors on the Internet.

We suggest that individuals without compatible Microsoft Word processors use Microsoft WordPad to create text by voice and then transfer the results to OpenOffice or LibreOffice for final formatting. The text that is created can be used to prepare conventional documents, letters, reports, etc. including book formatting.

Accordingly, when we review speech recognition [Commands] we will use WordPad as our principal teaching tool, because the [Commands] used with it are the same as those used with the Microsoft Word processors 2002 and later.

For the most part whether using WordPad or compatible Microsoft Word processors, the text will be the same. Formatting the text with either OpenOffice or LibreOffice, will result in documents closely emulating those created by Windows Speech Recognition using those Microsoft Word processors.

Other Questions?

Other questions should come up. Why don't we know more about it? How does it compare to commercial versions? Is FREE any good? These all fair questions.

First, producers of commercial applications conduct extensive advertising campaigns to sell their product. Microsoft has decided not to enthusiastically promote Windows Speech Recognition.

While millions use computers with Microsoft operating systems, only a small percentage of them are aware of and have experimented with Microsoft Windows Speech Recognition. Individuals and small-business owners with these operating systems, who recognize the benefits of speech recognition, but are unaware this application is on their system, are inclined to purchase a well-advertised version to produce text instead of Windows Speech Recognition.

Second, as we will see, Windows Speech Recognition has been favorably compared to commercial speech recognition programs by reputable organizations and individuals.

Why People Are Not Using Windows Speech Recognition

There are four main reasons people are not using Windows Speech Recognition. First, they don't know about it. Second, some discover it, have a compatible Microsoft Word application or WordPad, pick up an attached microphone, say a few words and expect a "Eureka" experience. It doesn't work that way. None of them do.

Third, owners of these systems without a compatible Word application do not realize that WordPad works well with speech recognition and last, some who use Word or WordPad, do not take the time to complete the Microsoft tutorials, or complete them but do consistently applied them. Without guidance, many run into problems and ultimately figure it's not worth the hassle. They either attempt to improve their typing skills, or simply resign themselves to continue using their "favorite" word processor and put up with the keyboard.

Experience with Speech Recognition

We experimented with speech recognition before we discovered it on the Vista operating system. The Vista application was superior to the ones we used earlier so we stopped using them and switched to Windows Speech Recognition. We have continued using Windows Speech Recognition since then on Windows 7, 8, 8.1 and Windows 10, on desktops, laptops, Surface, Tablets, and 2-in-1 computers.

We have bought and compared commercial versions of speech recognition with the Microsoft Speech Recognition Application. With several years' experience with Microsoft Windows Speech

Recognition, we concluded that for us, the command structure of Windows Speech Recognition was more natural and more efficient than continuing to use the commercial versions we tested.

Even though Windows Speech Recognition is free it recognizes a surprising number of words. It can be modified to accommodate even more by using the [Speech Dictionary] feature to add words unique to individual vocabularies, edit existing words, and prevent incorrect words from appearing in the text and on the monitor.

On Its Own Merits – TopTenReview

We have reviewed many comments about Windows Speech Recognition on the Internet, both favorable and unfavorable. One of the earliest favorable articles was written by TopTenReview in 2009. Vista was fairly new then. In an article *Got Vista? Voice Recognition is built in,* they made the following observations. The original link, is no longer posted, but the report below was found at:

http://www.toptenreviews.com/business/software/best-voice-recognition-software/got-vista-voice-recognition-is-built-in.html

> There are a couple of reasons why we were impressed with Windows Speech Recognition. The first is accuracy. Windows Speech Recognition transcribed voices to text faster and better than many of the stand-alone programs in this review. It kept up with normal words and it handled a lot of the jargon and uncommon words we threw at it.
>
> The other reason we were so impressed is the amount of features included in the software. The initial tutorial and voice training modules work well to set up the program to adjust to your voice, and from there the software continually improves results as you use it. The commands are numerous enough they're hard to remember at first, but once you become accustomed to them they become a real asset.

This echoes our observation. We are convinced, however, that many are still unaware of it, and for that matter, many are not aware of speech recognition at all; although an increasing number are familiar with how it is used with cellphones and Internet search engines.

How Does It Compare to Commercial Programs?
Top 10 Review's Dictation Test

In another post TopTenReview created and conducted a test that appeared on their website on April 28, 2009. They compared four commercial speech recognition programs. Since Microsoft Windows Speech Recognition was, and still is free, it was NOT one of them.

They tested these commercial versions using identical paragraphs containing 125 words and 15 punctuation marks. All of these were tested twice.

The best result they reported was 9 errors producing 98% accuracy, the second, 17 errors with 93% accuracy. The third application resulted in 19 errors, 92% accuracy. The last, a total of 34 errors, for an accuracy rating of 86%.

We Take This Test

We took the same test on three occasions. We completed it in June of 2012 using Microsoft Speech Recognition with Microsoft Word 2003, with 4 errors. We retested twice in July of 2014 using Windows 7/WordPad.

The first time we had 4 errors. The second time, using the same word editor, we had 6 errors. (We read two words wrong and had to count them as errors.) Even if our results were doubled, the results were still be favorable.

See the Appendix

With the permission of TopTenReview, we are printing a copy of the test they put together in the Appendix. Try it soon and in six months.

Another favorable review may still be on the Internet at: http://anewdomain.net/lamont-wood-windows-speech-recognition-vs-dragon-naturallyspeaking-shootout/

aNewDomain.net

We discovered another evaluation of Windows Speech Recognition authored and posted by Lamont Wood of aNewDomain.net in 2014. He used Lincoln's Gettysburg Address, which consists of 271 words and 43 punctuation marks. This is a document of 314 words when using dictionary words, not five-keystroke words. He has allowed us to include his results in this book.

He began his evaluation by first timing his keyboarding. Typing the Address took him a total of 475 seconds. After correcting errors this averaged 34 words a minute.

He then compared those results by composing the same material using a commercial speech recognition program, and then repeating it with Windows Speech Recognition. It took him only 159 seconds to compose the Address on a commercial version of speech recognition and a slightly longer 164 seconds with Windows Speech Recognition.

With the commercial program, he had 2 errors; 99.4% accuracy. After correcting those 2 errors, he had a throughput (output relative to input) of 74 words per minute.

Using Windows Speech Recognition, he recorded 7 errors, 97.8% accuracy; which after correcting the errors resulted in a throughput of 73 words per minute. In spite of more errors, a comparable result.

Results

We took the test using Windows Speech Recognition, first with WordPad/Windows 10. On our first attempt, we made the mistake of not first re-familiarizing ourselves with the Address. It took us 305 seconds, with 5 errors. We are somewhat handicapped mathematically, but this appears to calculate 98.4% accuracy with only 61.77 words a minute after correcting errors.

We took the test a second time, the next day, using Microsoft Word 2013, attempting to match Mr. Wood's speed and accuracy. We did not. We reduced our time however to 205 seconds. We were pleasantly surprised, however, that we had only 1 error with a corrected accuracy of 99.7% and something like 78 words per minute.

Check his site for more detailed information. Top 10 Reviews used Vista. We used Windows 7. We do not know what operating system Mr. Wood used. We used Windows 10.

Our Goal

Our first goal is to raise awareness of Microsoft Windows Speech Recognition. Second, is to present a tutorial to assist in learning and using it. Third, in addition to introducing Microsoft Windows Speech Recognition we are also introducing alternatives to Microsoft Word processors and other suggestions to present further options in creating documents.

There is an Alternative

Using speech recognition you will learn an easier way to create text that will not take any longer to learn than when you first learned to type. You have a very powerful free tool to make creating text easier, faster, and ultimately for most, more accurate than their best efforts at typing.

If you have a PC with one of the operating systems above, a functional microphone, Microsoft Word or WordPad and a full featured word processor; using good speaking habits, you can harness Microsoft Windows Speech Recognition without any cost other than this book.

We want to help anyone who experiences typing difficulties, or who wishes to improve the quality of their documents and increase their productivity. We are writing especially for students, who prepare numerous written notes and reports, anyone on a limited budget who produces documents;. such as small-business owners, without clerical staff, struggling writers, and anyone who has something to write, but is frustrated because of their lack of keyboarding skills.

For the benefit of these, we have also reviewed free applications that that will be of value in creating options to include with text, as well as suggestions on how to improve the quality of documents, organizing material and editing text.

Editing Capabilities

Depending on how well your message has been crafted, there is always the matter of reviewing (or editing) to discover and eliminate errors, or make changes in the text to further clarify your thoughts and make the result more readable. Speech Recognition enables the user to make these corrections by voice commands when the document is being prepared or when it is edited.

Editing "on the fly" saves time and improves the quality of the document. Don't forget that when we write something and review it we "see" what we THOUGHT we said, not what was actually put on the paper. We cannot avoid final editing and proofreading before submitting a final draft.

Learning Writing Skills

This is not a book on how to improve the quality of your writing skills. We will leave teaching those skills to others more qualified by education, experience and temperament. Creating more text provides the opportunity to use and perfect Windows Speech Recognition because experimenting, creating, editing and proofreading increases the number of new words and by its design adds them to the individuals User's Profile.

~CHAPTER ONE~

The First Key

If you use a PC with Microsoft Windows Operating Systems, Vista, Windows 7, Windows 8, Windows 8.1, or Windows 10 and have some experience with Microsoft Word, or another word editor or processor, it does not matter why you write. Even if you do not have a Microsoft Word processor, such as Microsoft Word 2002 or later, you can still use Windows Speech Recognition by using WordPad which is part of each of the Microsoft operating systems we have mentioned other than Surface 1 which already has Word 2013.

You also have access to FREE applications and programs that emulate costly programs. They either are on your computer, or can be downloaded for Free. How much better would your documents look if you knew about them and how to use them?

Windows Speech Recognition

We can talk faster than we can "type." Even if we intentionally slow our speech to concentrate on what is said, we can still talk faster and make fewer errors composing (dictating) than most of us can type. This is true of most people. It is true of us. Is it also true of you?

Technology has made unprecedented changes. Improvements in the quality and speed of computers, and the development of new devices have made this possible. Technological advances, marketing and distribution have greatly reduced the cost of desktop computers, laptops, Tablets, 2-in-1 computers and smartphones.

The First Step is to:
Stop Typing! …What?

Yes, stop fighting the keyboard. We will present a step-by-step guide that will help anyone wishing to significantly reduce his or her dependence on the keyboard. By carefully reading and practicing, typing will be reduced, and for some almost eliminated. Speed will increase and results will improve. We will introduce Microsoft Windows Speech Recognition and later three dozen or so other free applications and references any user, whatever their skill level, or need to write, will welcome as part of a new Writer's Tool Kit. They will help improve both "keyboard" efficiency and the quality of written materials.

Do Not Be Misled!

The two reviews, and many others, have provided favorable reports; BUT THERE IS A LEARNING CURVE. You need to be serious and make the commitment to spend time completing the interactive tutorials that are part of Vista and Windows 7 (but not Windows 8 and Windows 10), and the two other tutorials, which are common to all four operating systems. Sufficient practice is also necessary.

It will take time before you realize the maximum benefits of speech recognition. As you learn, however, and especially the more you use speech recognition, the more proficient you will become.

Making errors and learning from them is an important part of becoming skilled using this, or any new application. When you identify errors and know how to correct them, you can easily chart your progress. While testing, we have created and resolved many problems. Any user will find solutions for problems they encounter.

While Windows Speech Recognition does not work with just any word editor or processor, we have presented solutions for this problem for those who do not have or do not believe they can afford a compatible Microsoft Word application.

The cornerstone of this tutorial is Windows Speech Recognition, but we have expanded it to include information on additional free applications, programs and websites of interest to those who use the computer for creating text and more. Some of these are also Microsoft applications, but most are not.

We have strived to include free applications and programs. We have made some exceptions where some applications and programs are of exceptional value but are relatively inexpensive.

In a few instances, because of their superior utility, we have also included some applications that cost more, but with the exception of Microsoft Office 365, none of them cost over $100.00. We will give only a brief synopsis of these.

COMPATIBLE MICROSOFT APPLICATIONS
Microsoft OneNote

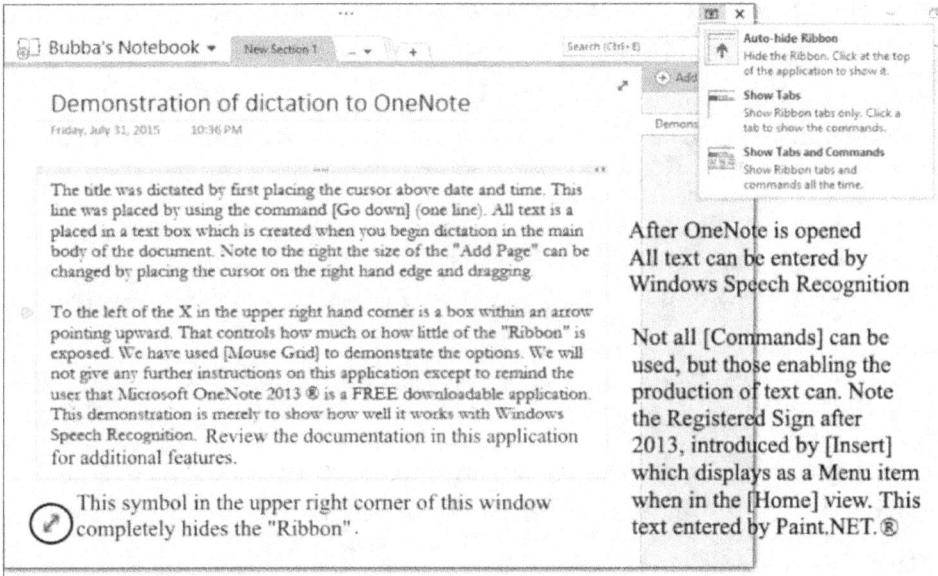

A popular application is Microsoft OneNote, which is also a free download from Microsoft. As its name suggests, it is an application for creating notes, but it is much more than that.

It is not a word processor, but it works very well with speech recognition. This application automatically saves entries. There is, however, no [Save] or [Save As...] option with OneNote. Contents however can be [Exported.]

Download it if it is not already on your computer or activate it, if it is. To add another page after it is set up, open the tab with the (+). The image on the last page is a composite of the features of OneNote and shows text that was created by dictation. For additional features download and experiment with it.

Sticky Notes

This little application is also compatible with Windows Speech Recognition. This works well if you want to make just a few notes as reminders, a To-Do List, or temporary storage for research. New notes can be created by clicking on the (+) in the upper [Left] corner. Several can remain open at one time. By [Coping] and [Pasting] content can be placed in word processors or editors.

Place its icon it on the Taskbar. Use the mouse to move them out of the main viewing area. When it is clicked all notes will be available or if displayed will be hidden.

Also [Hide] using [Alt] [F4]. To display again click on the icon on the Task Bar . To [Delete] individual notes use the Trash can in the upper [Right] corner.

WordPad / Microsoft Windows 7

Since not everyone will have a compatible edition of Microsoft Word, WordPad will be used as the model word editor for this tutorial. The Windows 7 version is representative of the operation of Microsoft Word processors and WordPad from Windows 7 to present.

WordPad in Windows 7 & 8 added the "Ribbon," which has been continued in Windows 10. With the "Ribbon," WordPad, Microsoft text editors, Word processors, and many Microsoft applications since the introduction of Office 2007, share a similar format.

WordPad/Vista

The basic structure and appearance of WordPad in the Vista operating system is similar to Microsoft Word 2002 and most other earlier word editors and processors. Although it differs in appearance, WordPad/Vista responds to the fundamental [Commands] and most of the advanced [Commands] of speech recognition. While Microsoft Word itself prior to Word 2002 is not compatible with Windows Speech Recognition it can be used to format text created with other Microsoft applications.

In CHAPTER EIGHT, we will discuss formatting choices available to those who use WordPad to create text. Learning how to use WordPad will also act as a primer for using Microsoft Word.

Setting up Your Word Editor/Processor

To learn the [Commands] and other features of Windows Speech Recognition use WordPad or a compatible Microsoft Windows Word application (Not earlier than 2002.) Setting up a page with narrow margins and an 8.5 by 11 inch canvas will be sufficient to complete the exercises that follow.

If you wish to format your editor or processor you can review CHAPTER EIGHT, but any compatible word editor or processor can be used for these exercises without any special formatting.

Except for some few specialized [Commands] of some Microsoft Word processors, those using WordPad will experience the same results as those using Microsoft Word.

If intending to produce text with WordPad and transferring it to either Microsoft Word prior to 2002, OpenOffice or LibreOffice, it will not be necessary to format these word processors now. All of the following exercises will be conducted with a compatible Microsoft Word application or WordPad.

If you create documents in later Microsoft Word applications, reviewing them in earlier Word applications can distort the formatting so don't for instance go from Word 2013 to Word 2010.

~CHAPTER TWO~
How it Works - A Non-Technical View

In brief, when using Microsoft Windows Speech Recognition, like all speech recognition applications, it is constantly monitoring to determine whether spoken words are first [Commands], or second, text. When it determines which, it responds accordingly.

Simplified Illustration of the Process

Risking oversimplification, a speech recognition application converts words spoken into a connected microphone into audio signals. These are either matched to templates, stored in the speech recognition application as [Commands] or words and phrases and will then execute a [Command] or create text.

A large amount of data is already in the speech recognition application stored in memory "A." Additional data is added to the User's Profile and the database when the Microsoft tutorials are completed and additional words are continually entered using the application. When activated, they interpret the signal either as a [Command] or as text.

When the user speaks into microphone "B," the signal goes to the engine "A," which searches the database. If there is an exact match, it recognizes it first as a [Command], or if it is not a [Command], as a character, word, phrase, or sentence; and causes the word processor or word editor to display it on the monitor "C."

Dictation continues. If an incorrect match is made the user can [Correct that] to repeat the request. Several possible "matches" will be shown on the monitor in the [Alternates panel], shown below. If one is correct, the number corresponding to it is said and acknowledged with "OK." Dictation then continues.

If still incorrect, the user can respond with "Spell-it," which we will discuss later, and proceed to spell it. When the correct word is spelled the change is "OK'ed" and dictation resumes.

When the Microsoft tutorials are completed, the application personalizes the responses and words are added to the database. Words and the user's speech characteristics are also added to the User's Profile. Because it is responding to a specific voice and how words are spoken, it is important that words be clearly spoken and the speaker refrain from inadvertently saying [Command] words in isolation.

Not a "Sleight of Hand" Application

As when learning any new task, speech recognition requires a commitment and practice. By analogy, one does not learn how to play the piano or guitar by simply buying one, bringing it home, and with a "magic book" start playing beautiful music. They begin following instructions, in printed form and hopefully also from a competent instructor. After careful study and practice, they begin creating music. It may not be your genre, but if done correctly it will be acceptable, and in some cases even exceptional.

Many people buy a guitar, learn to form some basic chord patterns, learn a few songs and start enjoying progress. After a while, for many, other things become more important and they play less and less and lose much of what they have gained. They may resume and become more proficient, but continued playing and practice, practice, practice are essential to advance as far as possible

Others become discouraged, or lack enough incentive to practice and before long the skills diminish. Until there is a commitment and practice, practice, practice, no improvement can be expected.

Windows Speech Recognition takes no longer to learn than typing on on a keyboard. Determination and continued practice are the keys to improving either of these skills. First you learn it, and then by careful, accurate and frequent use you continue to perfect it.

We did not always get the anticipated results. This prompted us to analyze the problem and either correct what we were doing wrong, or if the application or the computer was creating the problem, to find alternate ways of dealing with these glitches. Part of learning is not only learning what to do, but also learning what not to do.

Recognizing and resolving problems maximizes the benefits. Other than a poor microphone or a sluggish computer, the No. 1 reason for errors, other than failing to practice is poor speaking habits. Always concentrate on speaking clearly into a well-positioned microphone.

The application will work for you if you are serious and spend time to learn it. Many people who could benefit from it, without additional guidance become frustrated, disappointed and give up. We wrote this tutorial to encourage them.

Now, if you are interested in improving or expanding the usefulness of your computer, Windows Speech Recognition will repay you for your time and patience. Each time you use it, and the more you use it, the more efficient you will become.

If you are simply curious but not convinced, open Microsoft Windows Speech Recognition, complete the Microsoft tutorials, open a compatible word processor and begin dictating. You may be surprised how well you do. When you understand the [Commands] with additional practice you have a new improved method of writing.

THREE ESSENTIAL REQUIREMENTS

Compatible Processor

Windows Speech Recognition requires using a compatible word editor or processor such as Microsoft Word after 202, or WordPad.

A Compatible Microphone or Headset

Many new computers have internal microphones that are adequate, however, they lack the directional qualities of desktop microphones or headsets, but in a quiet environment, they will work. Failure to speak clearly and use an adequate microphone will almost always guarantee disappointment, discouragement, and poor results. If your computer has a quality microphone, you will not have to make any immediate investment, unless you wish to upgrade, other than the cost of this tutorial.

Desk Top Microphones

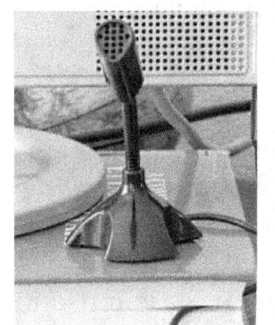

If your computer does not have a built-in microphone, or one that is inadequate, it is essential that you buy a microphone or headset that is speech recognition compatible. Headsets are available and can be purchased online at Amazon.com, Ebay.com, or elsewhere for under $20.00 including postage. Match the connecting cables with your computer.

A desktop microphone works far better than we anticipated. They are very small but responsive. It is currently being sold on eBay for between $5.00 and $7.00, including shipping. The obvious advantage to using a desktop microphone is that you are not encumbered and restricted by a headset and it can be repositioned to increase its usefulness. Results will always be better if the environment is free of extraneous noises.

Speak Clearly

Assuming your computer is operating efficiently, you must first concentrate on speaking clearly, and for many, slowly at first; as if every word counts, (Because it does). Experiment talking like a radio or television announcer.

Some reviewers say you should simply talk naturally. Our experience is that this does not work well at the beginning. One should consciously continue to improve their delivery. Experiment on how you pronounce words and what cadence works best for you. Certain combinations of words, word endings and similar sounding words require more concentration.

The application works better at recognizing words in phrases than individual words. This is because the application associates some words with others. But many words have similar sounds. For example, the words to, two and too and the numeral 2. The same is true of for, four, fore, and 4. Accordingly these are often produced in error. Words that seemingly do not sound alike are not always correctly identified, such as "and," "end," and "in."

The application has to "guess" the best match. Part of the challenge is recognizing what words or phrases the application has a problem interpreting, anticipating them and working around them.

After learning the fundamentals, with practice, the user will learn to minimize these problems. Speaking in phrases, using a combination of words, even when not needed in a sentence, and deleting some of them to get the correct response, is part of the learning process. To be aware of this is to be one step up.

~ CHAPTER THREE ~

Introduction
To
Microsoft Windows Speech Recognition

OK – It's all New

The Concept – This is a Tutorial

A tutorial is a method of transferring knowledge by systematically developing a subject. The goal is to provide sufficient information on a subject to enable a student not only to understand it, but also to apply what has been taught.

Learning any new discipline, and especially a multifaceted application such as speech recognition, is cognitive. That is, the process of acquiring knowledge by reasoning, intuition, perception, and especially by doing. Accordingly, learning speech recognition is not just learning a few [Commands], saying a few [Command] words and producing a "Eureka" document with minimal effort.

Rather, it requires learning and using the correct [Commands] of speech recognition, then practicing and applying them to successfully create documents. This involves using voice [Commands] to produce results formerly accomplished with the keyboard and mouse. Some tasks, such as locating files on devices and drives, while possible, are often more efficiently done with the mouse.

This tutorial has been created for people who have some knowledge of computers, word processors and who are at least familiar with keyboards; and frequently use them to produce a significant volume of documents, sometimes even for publication.

We are structuring this tutorial, however, to reach both the experienced and inexperienced, the prolific and the occasional writer. Even if speech recognition is not of interest, we will present other resources that many are unaware of and can be successfully integrated to produce or enhance documents.

Application vs. Program

Microsoft refers to Windows Speech Recognition as an application. If you inadvertently call it a program, it is not going to crash your computer. On the street, most people would probably consider this application a program.

Speech Recognition Is Speech-to-Text Conversion

Speech recognition and speech-to-text conversion refer to the same process. They enable composition of text by voice using a speech recognition application and a word processor that responds to the electrical conversion and creates text that is displayed on the monitor.

Speech recognition first "listens" for [Commands] to determine if it should perform a specific predefined function it is programmed to recognize. Second, if no [Command] is recognized it converts what it "hears" to text.

An essential element to successfully using speech recognition is, understandably, the development of good speaking patterns that are clearly "understood" and "interpreted" by the application.

A new Windows Speech Recognition user, after completing the Microsoft tutorials concentrating to use careful speaking techniques, could compose straight text without giving any [Commands], other than punctuation and line breaks.

Editing is a Significant Advantage

They would, however, ultimately encounter unintended results. Windows Speech Recognition [Commands] permit the correction of errors, or the editing of text "on the fly." With experience, a user will learn what [Commands] to use to create and edit text as they go. They can then make necessary changes in a document as they continue to create and edit text by voice. After learning speech recognition, users of speech recognition can create documents with minimal use of the keyboard and mouse.

Speech Recognition is Not Voice Recognition

Speech recognition and voice recognition are separate disciplines and are not to be confused. The latter uses the interpretation of spoken wave patterns to identify a specific person, in much the same way fingerprints or DNA identify specific people.

Not Automatic

For speech recognition to efficiently evaluate data, it must have significant exposure to a speaker's vocabulary and the speaker's manner of speaking. The more the program is used the better it "understands" and "interprets" [Commands] and accurately converts words which are not [Commands], into text.

After learning speech recognition users will realize they can work much faster and produce text more accurately by voice than they can type. Also because everything is done by [Commands], correcting errors and editing can be done immediately. Another benefit is that it enables those who have limited physical dexterity to use a keyboard, to confidently and efficiently create documents on a computer.

[Commands]

When Windows Speech Recognition is running, it is continuously "listening." For that reason it is important learn all the essential key [Commands] and to reduce "noises" to maximize the use of the application.

We have observed what has worked for us and what has not. Also, what alternate [Commands] are available to perform the same or similar functions. We have searched for alternate solutions. Finding answers, we continue to further improve performance. We are presenting step-by-step, our observations and tips on how to more easily learn and effectively apply this application.

Preview - Commands – Alternatives

Not every [Command] and (Subcommand) available in speech recognition will work in the same way, with every user, or with every computer. But there are many ways to accomplish the same goal.

Where a specific [Command] might work well for one person with a word editor or processor, an alternative [Command] may work better for someone else using another computer. Our motto is, "If you can't find THE way to do something, use an ALTERNATE way."

Let's begin with a brief explanation of how [Commands] will be displayed in this tutorial when they are within a sentence, as opposed to when they are in a Table or a Quick Guide.

[Commands] (Subcommands)

First, we will present the [Command] followed by the (Secondary command) and when applicable the (third, or tertiary, part of the command). The initial [Command] will be shown in [Brackets] the secondary and following (Subcommands) will be in (Parentheses).

When introducing the application, examples will be given of [Commands] and how they work. For now, do not be concerned if you do not fully understand how the [Commands] work. We will discuss them individually in more detail later.

Preview Examples

Some [Commands] consist of four parts such as [Go] (Back/ Forward) (# of Characters) or (# of Words), [Go] (To End of) (Beginning of) (Sentence/ Paragraph/ Document). Others have only two parts such as [Open] (WordPad). When you see a forward slash

(/) between two words in [Brackets] or (Parentheses), you have a choice between them. Do not say the words [Brackets], (Parenthesis) or (/) forward slash), or both of the (Subcommands) divided by a forward slash (/) at the same time. Choose and say only one.

For example with (Back/Forward) use (Back) or (Forward) but not both. When you see the character (#), this represents the number of Units the program is to execute. This can be expressed in characters, letters, words, phrases, sentences and paragraphs.

Example: [Go] (up four paragraphs) or [Go] (back three words) would be expressed in this tutorial as [Go] (Up/Down) (# of Units) and [Go] (Forward/Back) (# of Units), with the user inserting the correct variables of the (Subcommand).

MAXIMIZE LEARNING

To avoid frustration and develop confidence as you begin Windows Speech Recognition, do not be discouraged if you make errors. When we begin any new task, we learn from our successes and our failures. Follow instructions and apply what has been presented.

We learn from correct, incorrect responses, as well as from unanticipated ones. Correcting errors reinforces learning. So learn from your mistakes. Even with the best instructions, we do not "own" new skills until they become automatic. Do not be discouraged when errors are made.

Analyze mistakes. They may follow a pattern. Identify the result and why it occurred. Windows Speech Recognition provides [Commands] and alternate [Commands] to work around them. Do not despair. Help is built into the application.

If there are significant interruptions you may find text is still being created, or when you attempt to resume, it will stop responding. If you need to take time to think about what you are going to say, or when you're being interrupted turn speech recognition [Off]. Turn it back [On] when you are ready and continue your composition.

If you do not have one of the compatible Microsoft Word processors on your computer use WordPad as your principle processor. All versions work well with Speech Recognition. You can always [Cut] and [Paste] what you have created into a finishing word processor. We have mentioned OpenOffice and LibreOffice, but data can be transferred to many other full featured word processors.

Best and Worst Practices

Two of the most important [Commands] are [Save] and [Save As]. Be careful using the [Commands] [Select] (all) and [Delete] or [Delete] (all). Never use them in a sequence. They will do exactly that. They will select what you have created, from a single page to an entire document and you will end up with only a blank page.

If you want to [Delete] the word "all" never use the combination of [Delete] and (all). It will be interpreted as [Delete] everything in the document. While [Undo/Undo that] will usually salvage it, it is not infallible. Later, we will introduce better ways to isolate words for [Deletion]. Until then form the habit of regularly [Saving] your work both to the computer and also to an external USB or Micro SD.

The Unexpected

When something unexpected happens, and the application hangs up, do not despair. There is a reason for it, but you do not need to know how to correct it now. The first thing to do is to [Save] your work.

When it happens, make a note of what you were doing when it happened. Rather than going through the frustration of trying to understand it, shut Speech Recognition down, restart and continue.

If you get the message "Command cannot be performed," first try giving the [Command] [Cancel that] or [Cancel]. Try it several times. If unsuccessful, turn Speech Recognition off and then back on. If it does not clear, [Save] your work and open the [Task Manager]. It opens by holding down [Ctrl] and [Alt] then [Delete]. Just opening the Task Manager often will clear it. If it does not, use the [Task Manager] to close the document. Reopen and continue.

Speech recognition sometimes will not recognize a word, especially when a single word is spoken in isolation. It will more likely recognize a word if it is in a phrase. For instance, the word "add" is often confused. But if you use "add another word," by [Deleting] the last two words "another word" you can get "add" without having to repeat it several times or having to spell it.

Speech recognition makes better choices if what is said is put in context using associated words or phrases. It is easier to [Delete] extra words than to continue trying without success to get "the" word. We will discuss this in more detail when we discuss [Commands] and (Subcommands).

Often, when Windows Speech Recognition has been running on Windows 8 and Windows 10, when it is [Closed] or [Exit] is used, it will not start it up again. Try it once or twice. Doesn't come up? [Save] your work, then shut down and reopen the computer. No use wasting time trying to open it. It is more important to get the task completed than to unsuccessfully try to correct the problem.

Enable Dictation Scratchpad

This application permits the insertion of data into an application that

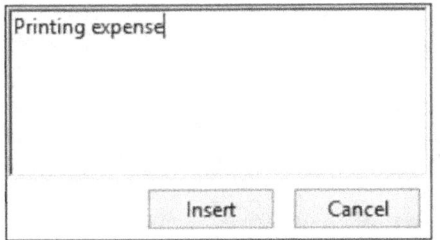

does not otherwise accept Windows Speech Recognition. Text is first composed (dictated) and it shows up in the scratchpad box. By using [Insert] the data is placed in the non-compatible application. Occasionally, however, without prompting the application will go into the [Enable dictation scratchpad] mode. It will start creating text in a box. Use [Cancel] or [Cancel that]. If this does not work, turn speech recognition to the off position. Turn it back

[On]. If it does not correct it, [Save] your work, [Close] it. Shut down your computer and [Start] over. While this happens very rarely, be aware of the possibility.

Improving Word Selection

If you have difficulty with specific words, changes can be made by adding, preventing or changing words using [Open Speech Dictionary]. If the application does not recognize what is being said, you have several options. This is one of them, which we will discuss later. There are several others, but when the application stubbornly refuses to produce a word, this feature can be used to manually create the word . Odds are the application will then recognize the word. One does not have to be a programmer to use this feature.

Windows Speech Recognition has sufficient [Commands] and words to meet nontechnical users' needs. Being able to add additional words or phrases improves efficiency and specialized words can be added to the User's Profile to make it more responsive even to highly individualized vocabularies, like law and medicine.

~ CHAPTER FOUR~

Microsoft Windows Speech Recognition

Set Up Procedure

Vista and Windows 7

To prepare Microsoft Windows Speech Recognition for first time use with Vista or Windows 7, click on [Start]. Then open the [Control Panel], [Ease of Access], followed by [Speech Recognition] which will open to [Configure your Speech Recognition options].

Windows 8

To simplify we will continue to refer to Windows 8.0 and 8.1 as Windows 8. Begin with the [Start] screen or the [Charms Panel]. Both have the [Search] (magnifying glass). Search for the [Control Panel] and follow the same steps as with Vista or Windows 7.

Windows 10

With Windows 10, there are several options. The easiest to remember is [Right click] on the [Window Icon] on the screen, scroll up and click on the [Control Panel] or (Search) for it and follow the steps above.
If Cortana is installed you can also use the [Command] "Hey, Cortana". When she responds with [Listening…] use, [Open] [Control Panel]. Follow the same steps as for Windows 8.

Although there have been some significant changes in Microsoft operating systems over time, they have had little effect on how Windows Speech Recognition responds to a [Command].

Following are the steps used to set up Window Speech Recognition. There are more than thirty items. Before yelling, "help," follow this procedure. It is easier to set up than it first appears.

SETUP PROCEDURE SIMPLIFIED

To set up Windows Speech Recognition, first go to the [Control Panel] followed by [Ease of Access] and [Speech Recognition] which will open the window below, which is the [Configure your Speech Recognition experience] window. Start with [Set up microphone] which we have marked with a ★ [Star] on [Configure your Speech Recognition experience image below].

This will open the [Microphone Setup Wizard]. This will ask for the type of microphone used. Selected the type used. This will then ask to repeat a sentence [Peter dictates to...pen and paper.] When completed select [Next]. This will indicate that your microphone has been set up. [Finish]. Reopen the Control Panel.

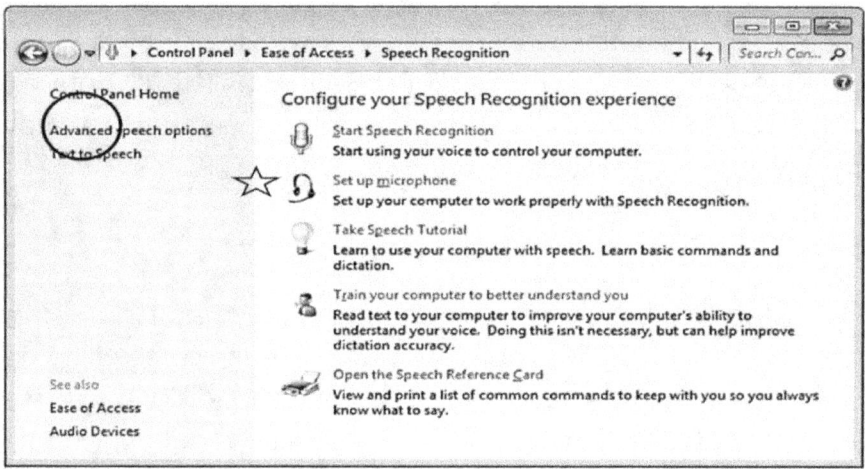

Proceed then to the upper [Left] corner and click on [Advanced speech options]. This will open the [Speech Properties] window.

[Speech Properties] Window

The [Speech Properties Window], shown on the next page, is where the majority of the [Speech Recognition] settings are made. There are two tabs on that window. Select [Speech Recognition]. We will not concern ourselves with the other, [Text-to-speech] tab.

There are a number of settings to consider on this window. Study them carefully because they will determine how well speech recognition will respond.

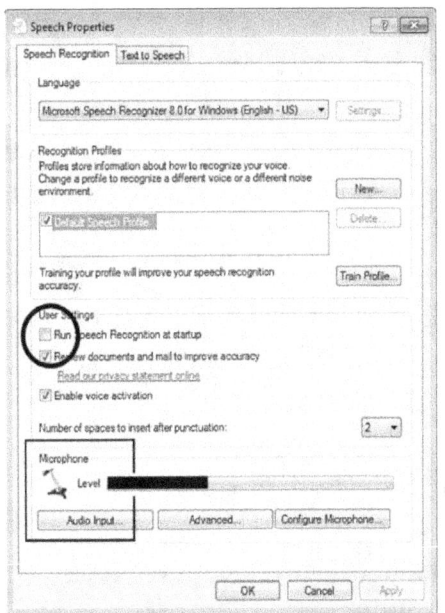

Give some thought to whether you want Speech Recognition to [Start] when you first turn on your computer or if you want it to open in the [Off] position. We find it more manageable. to set it to [Off].

Click on [New]. This will open [Add a profile] and [Profile]. Create a User name. Include a date with the username. For example, "Profile 9 12 21." (Do not use the quotation marks). With experience, over time you may wish to create a new profile to correct problems.

Complete all of the items on this window including [Train Profile]. That will open up [Welcome To Speech Recognition Voice Training]. If this is selected on Vista or Windows 7, it will bypass the interactive tutorial which is opened on [Take Speech Tutorial].

See additional information on the Microsoft Vista and Windows 7 tutorial in the next chapter.

If working with Vista or Windows 7, come back and complete [Take Speech Tutorial]. This also adds data to the User's Profile. On Windows 8 and Windows 10, this will open up a link on the Internet, showing two videos.

After completing them, come back and complete [Train your computer to better understand you] (Two Programs). Do both of them to build up the User's Profile. Then come back to Speech Properties and continue.

User's Settings - Run, Review and Enable

[Run Speech Recognition at startup], which we have circled, will open the application after your password is accepted. We do not use this. Experiment with it. Check [Review documents and mail to improve accuracy]. This will help improve accuracy using your own vocabulary.

[Enable voice activation] also is an option. It allows the application to [Open] and close by voice commands. Inactive it will show the message [Sleeping]. It will open with the [Command] (Start Listening). We usually do not select this either. We restart manually.

Important Step - Setting up the Microphone

If the volume is set too low, the application will not properly respond to the user's voice. If it is set too high, it will create distortion or pick up extraneous noises. Adjust this to determine the best level for you.

To set this, go to [Audio Input]. See image on the last page. We have placed a rectangular box around this. [Left] click the [Audio Input]. This will open the window [Sound]. [Left] click on [Recording]. Select the image of the microphone you are using and [Left] double click it. This will open the [Microphone Properties] Click on [Levels].

Microphone Levels

Set the slider, shown in the image on the next page, somewhere in the 70s or 80s. Experiment with the setting to determine what level works best for you. To check levels in the future, remember these settings are found on [Speech Properties] on the [Control Panel]. The microphone volume is also displayed on the Speech Recognition Control Module. See above image.

It is located to the [Right] of the microphone, which is inside the circle. It will appear as a blue indicator, and will move up and down from the bottom to the top while you are speaking. If you experience low readings, or get unexpected distortions, go back to [Microphone Properties] and readjust the volume either up or down.

If there is no movement check the microphone connection and the settings. If it cannot be resolved by adjusting the properties, try another microphone or headset. Hopefully the problem is not your computer.

We set the slider in the 70s or 80s. Experiment with it. On Windows 10 there is another setting, [Microphone boost]. Adjust this if necessary. You may need to come back to this several times when first learning this application. It is imperative that your voice be heard and that you speak clearly. Following these steps, complete the tutorials. The key to learning this application is to know and use the [Commands] and practice, practice, and practice.

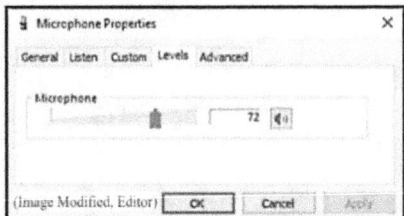

~ CHAPTER FIVE ~
Introduction
To
Microsoft Windows Speech Recognition

The "Message Board"

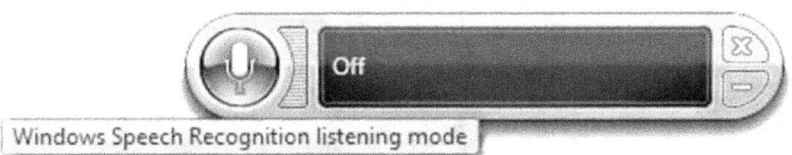

To follow this chapter [Open] (click on) the Windows Speech Recognition Module with a [Right] click of the mouse. The spoken [Command], is [Show Speech Options]. We call it the [Message Board], which is also known as Speech Recognition Control and Speech Recognition Module. If confused use the Microsoft name.

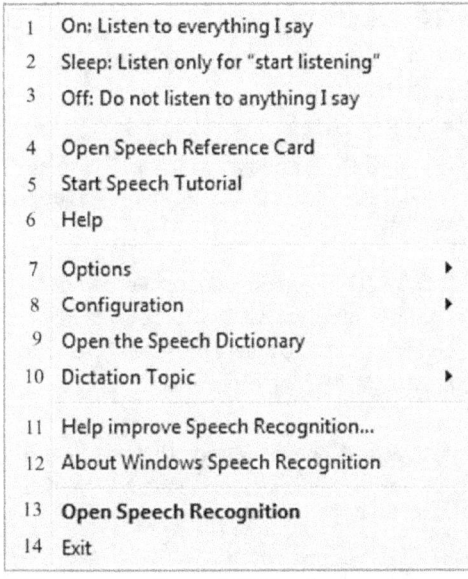

It is the same for Vista, Windows 7, Windows 8 and Windows 10, but as we will see, Vista and Windows 7 help screens are part of their operating systems, whereas, Windows 8 and Windows 10 open up help screens on the Internet.

After we describe some of the menu items, experiment with each of the topics so you are familiar with the variables.

On the next page we present the Quick Guide – Speech Recognition Module, where we summarize the contents of most these menu items. We do not cover them all. Review them.

Quick Guide - Speech Recognition Module

[Show Speech Options] can be opened with that command or a [Right] click on the Speech Recognition Module in all four operating systems.

On: Sleep: Off: 1, 2, and 3. The first three items are the same for all operating systems Experiment to see which works best for you.

1	On: Listen to everything I say
2	Sleep: Listen only for "start listening"
3	Off: Do not listen to anything I say
4	Open Speech Reference Card
5	Start Speech Tutorial
6	Help
7	Options ▶
8	Configuration ▶
9	Open the Speech Dictionary
10	Dictation Topic ▶
11	Help improve Speech Recognition...
12	About Windows Speech Recognition
13	Open Speech Recognition
14	Exit

Key:
A Vista and Windows 7
B Windows 8 And Windows 10

4. A. [Open Speech Reference Card] Open after [Show Speech Options] and [Left] clicking on [Open Speech Reference Card].

Opens the [Windows Help and Support] Common commands in Speech Recognition on the Vista and Windows 7 operating systems..

4. B. In Windows 8 and Windows 10 goes to the Internet.

5. A. [Start Speech Tutorial] Opens interactive speech tutorial on the operating system.

5. B Windows 8 and Windows 10 goes to the Internet.

6. A. [Help] Opens [Window Help and Support] What can I do with Speech Recognition? On the Vista and Windows 7 operating system.

6. B. In Windows 8 and Windows 10 goes to the Internet.

7. A & B [Options] We are interested only in [Enable dictation scratchpad] which should be checked in all four operating systems.

8. A & B (Configuration)[Speech Recognition Control Panel]. Easiest way for users of Vista and Windows 7 to access the [Configure your Speech Recognition experience].

9. A & B [Open the Speech Dictionary] will open with simply [Open Speech Dictionary] in all four operating systems

10. – 12 Skip.

13. A & B [Open Speech Recognition] returns to [Listening] Speech Recognition Module

14. Good-bye Speech Recognition

We have marked it A for Vista and Windows 7 and B and Windows 8 and Windows 10. While they use the same menu captions these two operate somewhat differently. Windows 8 and Windows 10 often go to the Internet for additional information.

If opening the Windows Speech Module by voice, use [Show Speech Options]. To open manually set the cursor in the black area, and [Right] click on the mouse. The first three menu items show how speech recognition will work when activated. Be familiar with all three options and select the one that works best for you. Once opened the menu line items can be navigated by voice using the [Command] [Go] (Up/Down) (# of Units). Here (# of Units) will be given as (number of lines). To open, give the [Command] [Enter].

For example after [Show Speech Options] to get to the second line use, [Go] (Down) (two lines). This will highlight the second line, Sleep: Listen only for "start listening," [Enter]. Any subsequent items would be selected by their line number and when reached, [Enter] will open that menu.

Vista and Windows 7 Tutorial

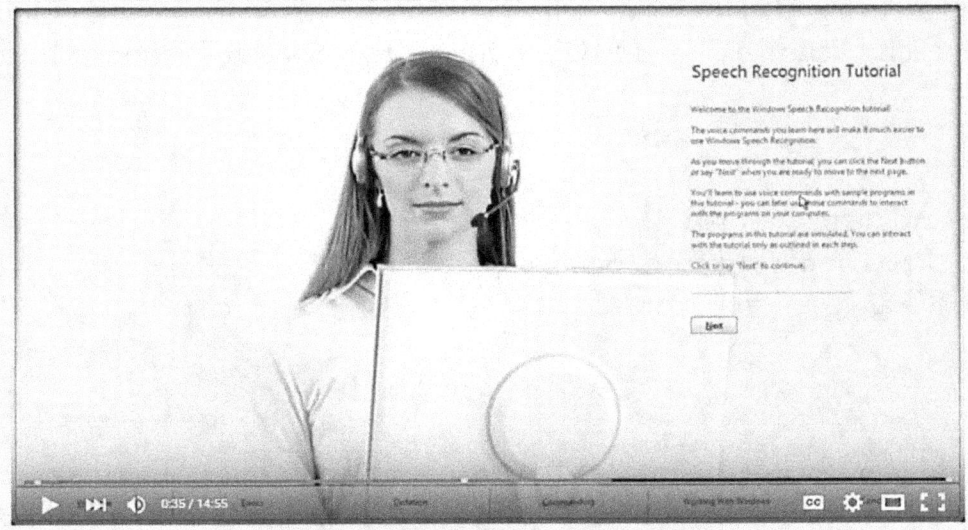

Line 5 A [Start Speech Tutorial]

We will expand upon Lines 5 and 9. Vista and Windows 7 present an interactive tutorial showing a young woman at a computer. This tutorial introduces many of the fundamental features of Windows Speech Recognition. Complete it on those two operating systems.

This tutorial gives an overview of the [Commands] available to Windows Speech Recognition. It also adds words to the User's Profile. This was discontinued and is not now part of the Windows 8 or Windows 10 tutorial.

This interactive tutorial often appears on YouTube. Search for it as "Windows 7 Tutorial" (Garage Geek Guy). While it is not inter-active, it is informative and first time users of Windows 8 and Windows 10 would do well to review this tutorial. Take notes and later compose (dictate) a summary of those notes on WordPad or Microsoft Word. The [Commands] and words will be added to the User's profile.

Line 9 A and B [Open Speech Dictionary]

This and the NATO Alphabet and Signs and Symbols which we will discuss later, are indispensable when getting the right word or spelling the right word seems impossible. It adds words, prevents words from being dictated and edits existing words. Open with [Open Speech Dictionary], and **NOT** [Open **THE** Speech Dictionary].

Speech Dictionary Options

1. Add a new word
2. Prevent a word from being dictated
3. Change existing words

Add a New Word

Add new words manually. If you try to enter them using speech recognition, it likely will not add them because it doesn't recognize them. Also if you leave Speech Recognition on when you type in the new words(s), chances are speech recognition will attempt to add additional words or characters. Accordingly, [Click] off speech recognition and type in the word, words or phrases.

After the data is entered, go to [Next]. When the next screen opens turn speech recognition back on to record a pronunciation of the word. Very clearly pronounce the word, and listen to make sure it is distinguished from other similar sounding words, then [Cancel].

Add a New Word

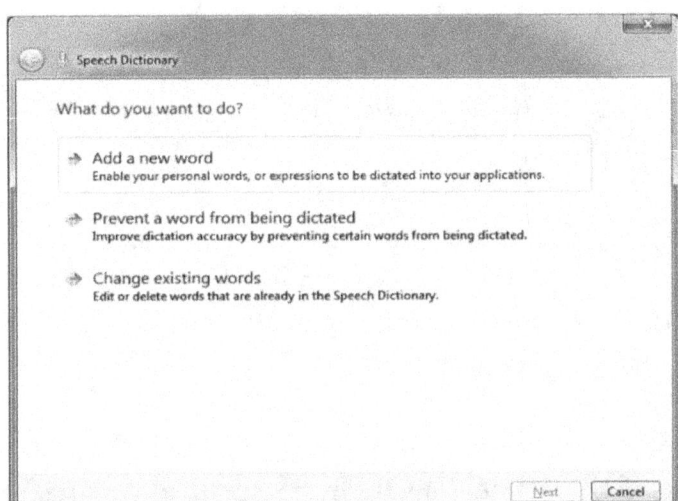

Mini-Macro Generator

While the heading says "Add (a) new word," it is not limited to one word. You can also use it to create word sequences, short phrases, technical terms, or to create templates, such as Internet user names like [john@gmail.com]. Type in as you would if sending an e-mail. Don't use the [ ]'s. When you [Record] record it as a key word such as "john's e-mail". When you want to produce it simply say "john's e-mail ". Try it also with your e-mail account, telephone number, or address. Identify them with key names.

This helps with phrases that are used often, and those that can be interpreted several ways. For example, we have often used the words Windows Seven. We would rather have the number 7 than the word.

To change that, we have used this feature to change the two-word combination to [Windows 7]. This opens up the possibility of increasing the accuracy of the application without having to use a more sophisticated application to create a macro. Setting up Windows Speech Recognition Macros which enables more complicated changes, will be discussed in a separate chapter. The series of words can also be created there.

Prevent a Word from Being Dictated

If a word is consistently incorrect, use the second part of this application to prevent it from being produced. Do this if the word is misspelled or if it is one of those words that keeps popping up when you briefly stop dictating.

As we suggested, many words cannot easily be distinguished because of their sound such as to, too, two and 2. Because they are not easily differentiated, they usually come up as alternates. The same is true of the words four, fore, for and 4.

You may find other words that the application has difficulty with. Make a note of them and flag them to see if alternates show up. If they become a problem, use the [Speech Dictionary] to add them.

Change Existing Words

Do not overlook the third option. You will be surprised what words can be found in the Speech Dictionary. Check this periodically to make changes, particularly if some words begin to give you difficulty. We discovered the application would return "dictionaries" instead of "dictionary." So we entered the word "dictionary."

Again, the [Command] is given as [Open the Speech Dictionary]. This does not work for us. We USE [Open Speech Dictionary].

This Ends Discussion on the Message Board.

REVIEW COMMANDS - SUGGESTIONS

The following [Commands] are reviewed in the tutorials. We include them here because of their usefulness. Some are also included in our Quick Guide Table 1 Column A on page 51.

[What Can I Say?]

1. (A) Vista and Windows 7. When selected, the feedback area will read [Showing Speech Reference Card.] This also opens the [Windows Help and Support] menu.

1. (B) Windows 8.1, Windows RT and Windows 10, will open [Showing Speech Reference Card] https://support.microsoft.com/en-us/help/12427/windows-speech-recognition-commands. (Might change.) See also our Quick Guide Tables.

[How do I do something?]

2. (A) Message will read [Searching for task…]. This brings up the [Windows Help and Support] window in Vista and Windows 7. It opens with a search box. Type in the subject you want explored. Also gives [Best 30 results for do something].

2. (B) For Windows 8 and 10 (Processing…Please wait) Opens up, https://support.microsoft.com/help/14213/windows-how-to-use-speech-recognition

[Move Speech Recognition]

3. (A & B) If the Speech Recognition icon is at the top of the screen using this [Command] will move it to the bottom, or top if it is at the bottom. You can also use [Hide Speech Recognition] and the reverse [Show Speech Recognition] to hide/return it.

Use this if Speech Recognition is hiding something on the monitor. Note: You can also move Speech Recognition with the mouse if you want to place it in a position other than the center of the screen at the top or bottom. Depending on what is on your monitor, you may find it more convenient to move it this way.

[Minimize or Maximize]?

4. (A & B) [Minimize Speech Recognition/Maximize Speech Recognition] is the same as [Hide Speech Recognition/Show Speech]. If you want to move Speech Recognition module off the monitor screen, use the first [Command].

To bring it back, use the latter. For the present, we would recommend that you not minimize it. You will want to observe the messages. If it is in the way, go ahead and move it. This concludes the use of the symbols (A&B).

Create Shortcuts and Bookmarks

Let's jump ahead here. After you've completed the start-up procedure and the tutorials, you can save time by a placing a shortcut on your taskbar. This is usually at the bottom of the monitor.

If you work between applications, for example, when editing pictures for documents, it helps to have your image editor on the taskbar, where it can be opened without interfering with the open window.

You can also switch between applications by using the [Command] (Switch Applications). Often it works better to [Switch to Desktop] first, then [Switch Applications].

Bookmarks - Internet Browsers

Most Internet browsers permit forming bookmarks. Many of them enable bookmarks to be placed at the top of the browser. This is convenient when working between Internet websites. To change sites, add a new Tab, and then click the bookmark for the other site.

How to Picture Yourself at the Microphone

Speech patterns similar to those of broadcasters, radio and TV personalities, work best with speech recognition. Being understood is a prerequisite for success in those professions. This is also true for success in using speech recognition. The application needs to "understand" the user's words and speech mannerisms if it is to properly interpret the message and properly distinguish and execute [Commands].

Key Commands

Pay attention to the [Commands] used in the tutorials. These are the KEYS to making immediate corrections. It is essential that your words be understood. Enunciation (how clearly you say your words) is important. But even if you are clearly understood, if you don't know the appropriate [Command], the application will not properly execute when you try to correct errors or edit.

If you find yourself composing (dictating) and the program consistently misunderstands Observe what the program does when you use the wrong [Command]. Make sure you are using the correct [Commands] and that your microphone is properly set up.

For Windows 8 and Windows 10

We have now covered the important differences of these four operating systems. The differences on the [Message Board] will become automatic if you upgrade your operating system.

The Vista/Windows 7 interactive tutorial was a great learning tool. Check YouTube for "watch windows 7 tutorial," currently by Garage Geek Guy for a posting of that tutorial. If you do not find it use other descriptive names on the YouTube search block.

~~DO NOT SKIP THE MICROSOFT TUTORIALS~~

Speech recognition already contains a large number of words and phrases it can recognize and reproduce, as well as [Commands] it recognizes to perform specific functions. Do not skip the tutorials.

If you find a [Command] simply does not work, try an alternative one. Speech patterns are unique to individuals. The program will interpret some of your words more accurately than others. Learn which present difficulties. If consistently incorrect, add, or delete them in the [Speech Dictionary].

For alternate [Commands], refer to our Quick Guides and [Show Speech Options] followed by [Open Speech Reference Card], which is found behind the [Message Board] on page 39 and also 40.

~ CHAPTER SIX~
Introduction
To
Quick Guide Table 1 Columns A&B

"Look Ma, no Hands"

Speech Recognition and More

Use one of the acceptable Microsoft Word application or WordPad to experiment with the principal [Commands] of Windows Speech Recognition and how they work together to prepare documents.

Allow us to share our experience with Windows Speech Recognition and follow a method we have developed which we believe will make it easier for you to learn. Ultimately, with practice using this tutorial as a guide, we will help train you to establish Windows Speech Recognition as your primary tool for producing documents.

A secondary objective, as we have mentioned, is to introduce you to FREE applications and programs which assist in producing better quality documents. Many of these are enhanced because they also work to varying decrees with Windows Speech Recognition.

We will demonstrate how to create tables, how to convert them to PDF files and how to copy those to produce image files which can be edited in an Image Editor. We will provide resources on editing and proofreading.

We also introduce an application designed by author and programmer, Simon Haynes, for managing scenes, characters, locations, items, and tools for writing novels or organizing complex reports. It is called yWriter6. It is part of a family of various applications designed by him.

Microsoft Windows Speech Recognition

The next several chapters deal specifically with Microsoft Windows Speech Recognition. We may at times call this a program. Microsoft, however, refers to this has an application. Before continuing with this chapter, we encourage you to review the last three chapters. Set up Windows Speech Recognition. Consult your notes on what was covered in the Microsoft Speech Recognition Tutorials, and spend a couple of hours practice. We will review all of the essential elements of speech recognition to make it easier for you to create a document.

Table 1 Columns A and B

When beginning this tutorial the reader should [Open] Windows Speech Recognition and an appropriate edition of Microsoft Word or WordPad. Experiment as we present new ideas. In our first Quick Guide, Table 1 Column A, we summarize in the first row how to set up and begin Windows Speech Recognition.

In the following rows, we will outline other details and [Commands] used in Windows Speech Recognition. We have also placed this and the other Quick Guides we have created in the back of this book to make them easier to find.

When we discussed the Speech Properties window, we reviewed the [Enable voice activation] box. If this is checked, the application will respond by showing "sleeping," To activate use the [Command] [Start Listening]. To close use [Stop Listening].

If you start it in the [Off] position start it manually by, [Left] click on the microphone in the circle on the [Left], close with [Stop Listening]. . Don't confuse the [Off] position with [Exit], which will turn speech recognition off.

Table 1 Column A and B

Table 1 Column A			Table 1 Column B		
Command	Action	Option	Command	Action	Option
[Start][Control Panel][Ease of Access][Speech Recognition]	To Access Application Create Shortcut	Complete all Microsoft Tutorials	[Press](Shift Key) (Individual Key) (Letters, Symbols or Numbers)	Duplicates Keyboard Entry	Numerous Secondary Commands
[Start Listening] [What Can I Say?][Show Speech Options]	Open Menu Message Board	Easy Access to Help	[Press] [Home] [End] [Alt][Ctrl] *Spoken Keystrokes:*	Up/Down, Keys Margins	One Unit {V}[Press] Command not Needed
[Open/Start] Word-Pad, Word, Excel, etc. [Close that]	Opens/closes Application or Program	{V} [File] [Press][Alt] (f)	[Go](Up/ Down) *(Line)* [Scroll] (Up /Down) *(Page)*	Navigation Up/Down By Line or Page	Increased Navigation
[Menu] (New) (Open)(Save/Save as)(Print)(Quick/ Preview)(Page Setup)(Exit)	Alternative [Application] Shows Files Under Menu. Items	{V} [File] Instead of [Menu]and [Application] [Press][Alt](f)	**Commands /Sub-Commands**		
[Show Numbers] [Switch to]	Numbers Menu Items Change Location	Alternative to File Name Location	[Delete] [Delete That]	(Word) (Next/Last/ Previous # of Units)	(Undo That)
[Mouse Grid]	Zeros in on Target	Isolates Specific Area of Window	[Correct] [Correct That]	(Word) (Next/Last/ Previous # of Units)	(Spell-it) (Start Spelling)
[New Line/ New Paragraph] [Enter][Enter]	Down 1 Line Down 2 Down 1/2	Alternate Command [Enter]	[Select] [Select That] [Unselect That]	(Word) (Next/Last/ Previous # of Units) (Word…Word)	(Unselect That)(Clear) (Arrow Keys)
Say Word not [Command]	Produces Word Not Action	[Spell-it] [Say Wrong Word, [Select] and [Correct]	[Go To] [Move To]	(Word) (Beginning of/End of)	(Word) (Sentence) (Paragraph)
Say a Word not [Number]	Produces the Word (One, Two etc. Not #)	[Spell-it] [Start Spelling]	[Go] [Move]	(Before/After) (Forward/ Back)	(Characters) (Word) (Sentence) (Paragraph)
[Numeral] – Get Number not Word	Produces Numeral not Word	[Press] Number Key	Take Second Series Speech Recognition Voice Training	Train Your Computer	Further Configure Your Computer

©ElCar Publishing August 2014 | Experiment with All Commands!

We prefer to leave [Enable voice activation] unchecked. For us, it does not respond well to [Start Listening]. For that reason, we want it [Off]. In addition, we often need to clear our thoughts before we resume.

When not composing for extended periods extraneous noises can cause it to produce letters or words. Turn it [Off] if you need time to organize. It is easy to turn it back on by clicking on the microphone. [Delete] any text added by background noises and continue.

[What can I Say?]

A reminder. With this [Command], Vista and Windows 7 will open with [Windows Help and Support]. It opens with a search window. If it shows [Hide all], click to [Show all]. This will show the [Commands] of Windows Speech Recognition. We will summarize the most important ones.

Windows 8 will open [Windows Help and Support] (How to use Speech Recognition) on the Internet. This will open two videos followed by [Show all] or [Hide all]. Here you have the option of watching the videos or selecting [Show all]. Watch the videos, then open [Show all]. Windows 10 will open with the Internet page [Windows Speech Recognition] [Commands]. Scroll down and click on [Show all]. This will display the [Commands]. Use [Show Speech Options] instead.

[Show Speech Options]

With this [Command], all the operating systems will open the menus behind the "Message board." For a review, see information shown on page 39 and 40. We have summarized some of these topics in Table 1 Columns A and B on page 51.

Open/Start

[Open] combined with a (Secondary command) (such as the name of an application) will open for instance your word processor or an other application. Follow with the name of the applications such as WordPad, Notepad, Word 2002, 2003, 2007, 2010, etc. This also opens browsers, Edge, Internet Explorer, Opera, Google Chrome, Mozilla Firefox, and perhaps other applications.

For Windows 10 users, Cortana may respond in the same way. Call her up by ["Hey, Cortana"] and [Open] (the name of the application). When she responds Speech Recognition will be suspended. They use the same microphone.

[Start] used without a (Secondary command) will open the [Start] menu of all operating systems. When used with a (Secondary command), [Start] performs the same function as [Open] (Google Chrome, etc.) Use whichever seems more natural to you to perform a function.

Using Cortana, you can also open Windows Speech Recognition and your word processor. When you first start using her she might misunderstand and might send you off to the Internet. With continued usage, she should open speech recognition.

Menu Can Be Collapsed

Under the caption [Menu] on the Quick Guide, we show (Secondary commands) that appear when [File] is opened. What is shown depends on the word processor being used.

The Ribbon on WordPad (beginning with Windows 7) can be shown

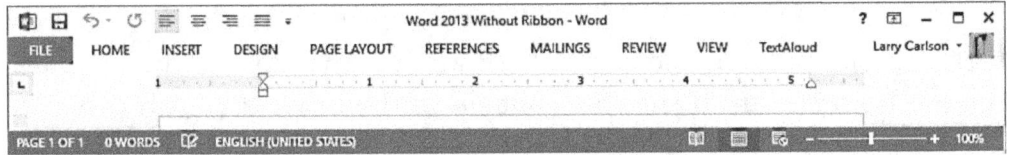

open or collapsed while preparing a document. The main menu items appear in the Show Tabs view. (Above). The items on the Ribbon continue to be available, but they are "behind" the main menu items.

If you are using WordPad other than Vista, or later Word applications, you can move some menu items to the Quick Access Toolbar for easier access. If you use them without the Ribbon, you will need to access one of the main Menu items to display the Ribbon options. You can then open them with the appropriate [Command].

Microsoft Word 2013 with "Ribbon"

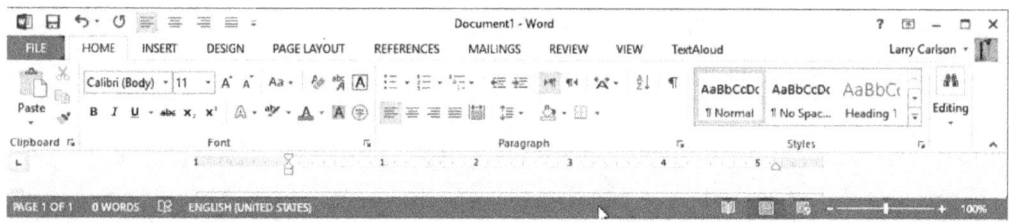

Note the five options that appear in the extreme upper [Right] hand corner of an open application [?] [□] [-] [□] or [x]. They are from [Right] to Left], Close, Maximize, Minimize [Box] controls what menus appears on the application, and [?] Word Help.

If you try to open any of the menu [Commands] [File], [Edit], etc. and you don't get the expected result, use [Show Numbers] instead, or as we will see later, other shortcut [Commands]. We will discuss this later, but this [Command] will place a series of numbers above menu items or over applications.

Table 1 Column A

Command	Action	Option
[Show Numbers]	Numbers Menu Items Change Location	Alternative to File Name Location
[Mouse Grid]	Zeros in on Target	Isolates Specific Area of Window
[New Line/ New Paragraph] [Enter][Enter]	Down 1 Line Down 2 Down 1/2	Alternate Command [Enter]

All of them will have a separate number. Observe that sometimes there are numbers at the top, bottom or on the side of the monitor screen. Ignore them if they are outside of the normal viewing area.

Select and say the number over the item you want to open. [OK] it and the item will open. Sometimes after the [OK] it will be necessary to use the [Commands] [Click that] or [Double-click that]. If it does not open use the cursor.

[Show Numbers] and [Mouse Grid]

If [Show Numbers] does not work, use the [Command] [Mouse Grid]. Consider these [Commands] as independent and also as partners. If one does not produce results, use the other one.

These are useful when opening menus when they do not respond to direct [Commands], such as open [File], [Save], etc., or opening links that appear after a search on the Internet. Use them as backup [Commands] if an application does not respond to a Primary Command. [Mouse Grid] seems to respond to its [Command] more consistently than the alternate [Show Numbers].

The Mouse Grid opens as a series of 9 grids. By selecting successive new grids by number, they continue to shrink into a smaller series of nine grids. Each covers a smaller area. When over the target area use the [Command] [Double-click] to open it.

[New Line] and [New Paragraph]

The first will, create a new line, the second will position a new paragraph. Some Microsoft word processors will advance only one line with the paragraph [Command]. To move down one line you can also use [Press Enter]. For a new paragraph, say [Press Enter] (twice).

[Say Word] not [Command]

During composition it is sometimes necessary to use one of the words the application uses as a [Command] word. If a [Command] word is activated unintentionally, depending on when it is said, it may respond by executing the [Command] associated with it. To avoid that, preface it with the word [literal]. Sometimes the word literal will print, when that occurs delete it.

We will discuss [Delete] in detail later, it is such a [Command] word. To use a [Command] word in a sentence preface it with [Literal] and then say the [Command] word. For example, if you need to use the word [Delete] at the beginning of a sentence you would say [Literal] (Delete). The word "delete" would appear as text.

Usually, if a [Command] word is said with several other words, especially in the middle of a sentence, the application will consider it as just another word and not treat it as a [Command]. It would therefore not be executed.

Since [Literal] is a [Command] word, to get the application to "type" literal, the [Command] is [Literal] (literal). If you want to use the word for a punctuation mark, such as period in the middle of the sentence, you must preface your [Command] by saying [Literal] (period), or [Literal] (question mark), etc. Say the punctuation mark at the end of a sentence as usual. [Literal] is not necessary for end punctuation.

[Say Word] not Number

If you want to show a word for a number rather than a numeral simply say the number; for instance, four, five, six. Sometimes the application will return a numeral instead of the word for a number. If that occurs say the number in a phrase, such as "six is half a dozen." [Delete] the unnecessary words.

Table 1 Column A		
Command	Action	Option
Say Word not [Command]	Produces Word Not Action	[Spell-it] [Say Wrong Word, [Select] and [Correct]
Say a Word not [Number]	Produces the Word (One, Two etc. Not #)	[Spell-it] [Start Spelling]
[Numeral] – Get Number not Word	Produces Numeral not Word	[Press] Number Key

Get Number not Word

If you need a number rather than a word preface your selection with [Numeral] and then say the number(s). For example, [Numeral] (76). If this [Command] gives you difficulty there are alternative methods to show numerals instead of characters.

As suggested, speech recognition has difficulty with the numbers 2 and 4, because of the homonyms to, too and two as well as 4, four, for and fore. Even using [Numeral] you may get one of the variations of (2) or (4) instead. In those instances, if you do not get them, use [Press] 2 or 4. If these numbers are the second or the third in a series, they may not create a problem.

Another way to handle numbers is to group them together such as saying "twelve, thirty-four," with the result 1234, or in the case of telephone numbers, beginning with (open parenthesis) followed by [Numeral], first three digits, (close parenthesis) followed by the [Numeral] and the next three numbers, a space, and then the [Numeral] again and the next four numbers. (623) 234 5678.

When you need a series of numbers such as those appearing credit cards group the numbers in a series of four separated by spaces. Or in the alternative try dictating them all in a stream to see if it works. You can separate them by creating spaces later. Anticipate potential problems using numbers. There is no guarantee. Speech recognition does not always get them right, but now you know a couple of techniques. Use them. Be innovative not frustrated.

[Press] (Name of the Key)

We have seen how the word [Press] works with numbers. It also works with keystrokes. If you use the [Command] [Press] (b), for example, you will produce a lowercase letter (b).

You could accomplish the same result by using the [Command] [Press] (lowercase) and then (the name of the key). But why? Unless at the beginning of the sentence, where it is most often capitalized, most words will be lowercase.

Individual Capital Letters

[Press Capital] and (the specific letter). The [Command] would be [Press Capital] (b). You would get capitalized letter (B). This can be used when including a middle initial between a first and last name. For example, John [Press] (Capital) (b) B [Literal] (period), then (Jones).

As we will see later, if the cursor is next to a word you want capitalized, use [Select] (Next/Last) (Character or Word). [Capitalize that] or [Lowercase that].

Repeat Characters or Letters

You can also repeat a character several times by giving the [Command] [Press] and the (character name) (number of times) such as [Press] (nine) (four times), with the result: 9999.

Or, although we don't know why you would want to, [Press] (b) (eight times) with the result: bbbbbbbb. (Count them.)

Duplicate other Keys on the Keyboard

You can also [Press] action keys, including, Insert, Home, Page Up, Page Down, Delete, End, Backspace, the four arrow keys, and, as we already know, the [Enter] key.

By using the [Press shift], and a letter character, you would get the same result as [Press capital] and a letter, such as B. Used over the characters above number keys you would get the symbol above them. Such as !, @, #, and $, for the number keys 1, 2, 3 and 4. Later you will see how you can carry that out by merely saying the symbol name, which is more efficient. (See page 72.)

Foreign Language Characters

We include here for general information only the availability of foreign language characters for Word 2013 and Windows 10. If an individual has a need to include foreign language fonts or words there are language options for Microsoft Word under [Options] and also in Windows 10 under [Settings]. Information is also available on the Internet both for fonts and keyboard maps.

In order to use them however one must have at least a minimal knowledge of or a translation of that language in order to successfully select the appropriate fonts and words.

In windows 10 go to [Time & Language] one can select from up to 111 different languages in alphabetical order by location including several local dialects. Under language from the listing there. Use the + sign and select a new language to add.

For other languages search the Internet for "foreign language keyboard maps" and the language alphabet fonts. See also: http://en.wikipedia.org/wiki/Keyboard_layout.

FUNDAMENTAL NAVIGATIONAL COMMANDS

We will now begin a discussion of the first of four fundamental navigational [Commands]. The first two use the [Command] (Press) followed by the appropriate key.

[Press] (Home) and (End)

[Press] (Home) moves the cursor to the [Left] margin. [Press] (End) moves the cursor to the [Right] margin. These [Commands] are simple, but helpful. Using them you can easily direct the cursor to either of the margins. Because [Home] is one of the menu [Commands], in Microsoft word processors, you must preface it with [Press] before saying, (Home). This may also apply when trying to get the cursor to go to the (End) as well. Experiment to see if this is necessary for (End).

[Go] (Up/Down) [Scroll] (Up/Down)

[Go] (Up/Down) [Scroll] (Up/Down) are two additional basic navigational [Commands]. The first enables movement of the cursor up-or-down by lines. If you use [Go] (Up/Down), the cursor will move by one line. If you specify the number of lines, depending on the size of the page, you can [Go] (Up/Down), perhaps 20 lines or so. [Scroll] (Up/Down) enables scrolling up or down by the number of page(s). To [Scroll] (Up/Down) less than a page use the [Command] without saying the number of pages.

Table 1 Column B		
Command	Action	Option
[Press](Shift Key) (Individual Key) (Letters, Symbols or Numbers)	Duplicates Keyboard Entry	Numerous Secondary Commands
[Press] [Home] [End] [Alt][Ctrl] Spoken Keystrokes:	Up/Down, Keys Margins	One Unit {V}[Press] Command not Needed
[Go](Up/Down) (Line) [Scroll] (Up /Down) (Page)	Navigation Up/Down By Line or Page	Increased Navigation

Both have limitations. Depending on the size of your page, it appears you can scroll up or down about 20 pages. Experiment to see how many lines and pages you can navigate by voice command.

SUMMARY

The above [Commands] and features are the part of the building blocks of Microsoft Windows Speech Recognition. At the beginning of the Table 1 Column B (Page 51) we have included, as a reminder, some of the [Commands] used in directing speech recognition. In the next chapter we will begin details of the [Commands] and (Subcommands) that perform what we refer to as the "Magic" of Windows Speech Recognition.

Before beginning the chapter, it would be well to take time to review what we have covered so far. Open a compatible word processor and practice composing. If you encounter problems with editing do not be concerned. We will begin to cover some additional techniques in the next chapter. Any experience you have will be helpful in understanding how Speech Recognition works.

~ CHAPTER SEVEN~
The "Magic"
Of
Windows Speech Recognition

"HOW DO YOU EAT AN ELEPHANT?"

Someone once asked the rhetorical question, "How do you eat an elephant?" For the fainthearted, we have no interest in eating an elephant, but it would present an interesting challenge. The answer is one "bite" at a time. Learning a new skill, like math and Window Speech Recognition, can at first appear to be a formidable task. But the answer is the same - one "bite" (not one byte) at a time.

Some people can learn a new discipline without breaking it down into its individual parts. Most of us, however, find it easier to learn if we break a new subject into "bite size" pieces.

The method in this tutorial is to do just that. Learning Windows Speech Recognition will not be as difficult if it is reviewed one step at a time. We have already covered a few fundamental [Commands] in Windows Speech Recognition. Open speech recognition and follow along. Do not expect perfect results when you first begin. As you practice, your results will improve.

1	[Commands]/ [Subcommands]

We are discussing Microsoft Windows Speech Recognition. We may at times refer to it simply as speech recognition. Understand that we are still referring to Windows Speech Recognition unless we indicate otherwise.

The "Magic" of Windows Speech Recognition is to produce text by voice, and also, to edit it by voice while continuing to compose. Let's leave the elephant analogy alone and instead use a much more familiar, and perhaps less controversial analogy similar to an eight-course meal. Let's take a few "bites," as we would from the cheese curds in this image, and discover the "magic" of Windows Speech Recognition.

We already set the table in Chapter Six where we presented the General Scheme. We also presented a brief introduction to [Commands] and (Subcommands). We have just completed two navigational [Commands] [Go] (Up/Down) (# of) lines and [Scroll] (Up/Down) (# of) pages. If we use the [Command] [Go] (Up) 10 lines or [Scroll] (down) 10 pages these [Commands] are useful, but not particularly "magical."

Overview of Commands/Subcommands
First Bite

A [Command] is a usually a single word such as [Delete], or a couple of words such as [Delete that]. We will refer to either of these as [Commands]. A (Subcommand) is a word or series of words that follow a [Command] to perform a more specific function. In this tutorial we will present [Commands] in [Brackets] and (Subcommands) in (parentheses).

For example, a [Command] we will cover later, [Go] (Forward/ Back) (# of Units), is a complex [Command] (Subcommand). The words in [Brackets] are the [Commands]. Those in (parentheses), whether one, or a series of words, are the (Subcommands).

 To use them, first say the [Command], in this example [Go], followed immediately by the appropriate (Subcommand). Let's assume we want to go ahead four words. The [Command] would be [Go] (Forward) (Four words).

In this chapter, we will study the functions of the most important editing [Commands]. First, we will look at the [Command] itself. Then, when it applies, we will include the addition of [that], which appears, for example, in the [Command] [Delete that]. This makes the action more specific. We treat this as a variation of the principal [Command], and cover it next. Finally, we will discuss how each Primary Command operates with associated (Subcommands).

Too Difficult?
Review the Command/Subcommand Table

At first, this may appear to be an overwhelming task. To make it easier, we have placed the subset (Subcommands) of the 5 major Commands in Column B. This Table has also been placed in the back of the book for quick reference.

	Commands/Sub-Commands	
1	[Delete]	(Word)(Next/Last / Previous)(# of Units)
2	[Correct]	(Word)(Next/Last / Previous)(# of Units)
3	[Select]	(Word)(Next/Last/ Previous)(# of Units) Word... Word)
4	[Go To] [Move To]	(Word)(Beginning of/ End of) (Next/Previous)(# of Units)
5	[Go] [Move]	(Forward Back)(# of Units) (Before/After)

Here, we have modified that subset for illustration purposes. We have numbered these five [Commands] and their (Subcommands). The reader should note that the first three Commands] have (Subcommands) in common. Once you grasp how they work with one [Command] you will already generally know how the other [Commands] using the same (Subcommand) will respond.

We will take each step one "bite" at a time. Familiarize yourself with this table. There's no reason to memorize it. After you have learned how they function, use the subset in Table 1 Column B (Page 51) as a reminder. There we have added a third column to include additional information that further explains action of each of these.

Commands/Subcommands

In this modified table we introduce in the second column the five most important [Commands] of Windows Speech Recognition. They are arranged beginning with [Delete] and ending with [Go]/ [Move]. The principal [Commands] are [Delete] [Correct] [Select] [Go to] and [Go]. The first three perform different results, but they function in much the same way.

(Word) (Next/Last/ Previous)

In column three are the (Subcommands). On the first line is the (Subcommand) (Word) (Next/Last Previous) (# of Units). This (Subcommand) is common to the first three [Commands]. Remember that (# of Units) refers to the number of letters, words, sentences, or paragraphs included in the (Subcommand). While items 4 and 5 contain some elements of the first three (Subcommands), they operate somewhat differently.

The First Three Major Commands

The first three [Commands] perform different functions. We will begin with their fundamental characteristics; then some of their more advanced operations when combined with the word [that], and finally when used with their (Subcommands).

Second Bite
[Delete] (Think Delete Key)

When learning, before using any of these [Commands], always make a point of observing where the cursor is located. The starting point of each [Command] is from the location of the cursor. One might think saying [Delete] would immediately edit the words just spoken. It does not. Think of the [Command] [Delete] as duplicating the [Delete Key] on the keyboard. On the keyboard [Delete] removes the next character on the [Right] → of the cursor.

	[Delete]
2	[Delete that]
	[Undo that]

When spoken as a [Command], it does the same thing. If there are characters or letters to the [Right] →, using the [Command] [Delete] will remove those characters or letters one by one, each time the [Command] is repeated. When the cursor is at the end of the last character on a line, if there is a word in the line below it, it will [Delete] the first character of the first word on that line. If there is no word on the line directly below but there is a new paragraph immediately below, it will first eliminate the space between the two paragraphs.

It will then start [Deleting] the characters in the next paragraph, beginning at the [Left] ← margin and deleting the first character of the beginning of the next word, then the second and so on until all have been removed.

When [that] is added, [Delete] takes on a new dimension. If you begin speaking a phrase and immediately realize it is not what you wanted to say, use the [Command] [Delete that] and the entire phrase will be deleted. Words to the [Left] ←, not included in the same phrase or sentence, will remain unaltered.

Again, where is the cursor? When a new phrase is composed, it will begin at the position of the cursor and extend to the [Right] → of it. When words are deleted, the cursor will return to the beginning position. This is the most common use of [Delete that]. As we will see, there are other options.

Change Your Mind?

If you said [Delete that] and decided that you wanted to keep what you had just composed, you would use the [Command] [Undo that]. It would reappear.

You could also use the [Command] [Undo that] instead of [Delete that] to accomplish the same thing and erase what you had just spoken. If you chose to use that and changed your mind, the corresponding recovery after this [Command] is [Redo that].

While [Undo that] is synonymous with [Delete that], we recommend using [Delete that]. It is more descriptive, and it avoids unnecessary confusion. Use the other [Command] if [Delete that] does not work well for you. This illustrates one of the ways Windows Speech Recognition provides alternate [Commands] to provide options to get the job done.

Hesitation

If we hesitate while composing a phrase or sentence, we create a new phrase with each hesitation. Then, only the last phrase would be deleted using [Delete that]. Anything composed before the last hesitation would remain unaffected.

Example:

[I think we need a new... ink cartridge.] In this example, if you hesitate after the word "new" and complete the rest of the sentence, and say "[Delete that]," you will have what we show below:

I think we need a new . . .

We are showing the hesitations by an ellipsis (. . .). If we hesitated as above, and then added a period after the word "cartridge," we would create three segments. Then only the (period) would be deleted with the [Command] [Delete that].

Directional Deleting
[Delete That] (Right]/Left)

When [Delete that] is used in an existing document, as opposed to a word or phrase just created, do not confuse it with using [Delete]. It is not limited to deleting characters only to the [Right] → of the cursor (ahead of it).

If the cursor is "resting" on the last character of a word, to the [Left] ← (behind) the cursor, and [Delete that] is given, it will remove that character or, if it is a word, the entire word.

Conversely, when it is "resting" against the beginning character of a word to its [Right] → it will [Delete] the character or word to the [Right] → of it. [Delete that] recognizes what it is next to. It will [Delete] an entire word, not just the first character, unless of course, the word is a single syllable such as (a) or (I).

To use, first determine where the cursor is in relation to the character or word. If before it, it will [Delete] the word to the [Right] →. If after, it will reverse its direction and [Delete] to its [Left] ←.

Inside a Word [Delete] Differs from [Delete that]

If the cursor is inside a word, the [Delete] will duplicate the action of the Delete Key and remove one character. Under the same circumstances with [Delete that], the word will be deleted.

The [Backspace] key works in reverse of the [Delete] key and when executed removes characters to the [Left] ← of the cursor one character at a time. We not concern ourselves with [Backspace], because, as we will see, there are alternate and better ways to do it.

WARNING a Reminder

The application occasionally will misinterpret [Delete that] used with a word and instead of deleting the word will DELETE THE PARAGRAPH OR ENTIRE DOCUMENT. Be aware of that possibility. **NEVER** use the [Command] **[Delete] (All)**, if the word you want deleted happens to be the word "all."

The application will execute the [Command] and the document will be deleted. The same would occur if you wanted to [Delete] the words "document," "paragraph," or "sentence," even if the word appears. It may not [Delete] the word but what the word symbolizes. We will show other [Commands] and (Subcommands) to deal with these situations. Do not attempt them now. [If you forget, you may be able to salvage it by using [UNDO THAT], but it does not always work.

Another safety precaution, is to not only [Save] your work to your computer, but also to a back-up USB drive. (Thumb Drive). Then in the event you have computer problems you can still salvage your work and if necessary continue working on it on another computer. It sounds like an unnecessary extra step, but if you have never lost a chapter or a document, you do not want to start doing it now. Analyze before deleting. Does all the phrase or sentence need to be deleted? Perhaps only one character, word or part of a phrase?

When [Delete] is used with other (Subcommands) shown in column two it has much more versatility. But first let's examine how [Correct/Correct that] works in its Primary Function.

Third Bite [Correct/Correct that]

Review the summary we just presented on [Delete/Delete that]. [Correct/Correct that] operates in a similar manner. Here the addition of [that] may have no effect. Using either may produce the same result. Instead of deleting what was just said, either [Command] would highlight it instead and open the [Alternates panel]. This will display several possible alternatives found in the database. It may not show what was spoken. In the example given on page 69, (1) was what was expected. Note the other possibilities.

| 3 | [Correct] |
| | [Correct that] |

Alternates Panel

[Delete] could have been used. One advantage of [Correct that] is that it provides a visual record of what was said and provides alternatives which the application has considered. First review all the other possible interpretations. If one is correct, the user need only say the number and [OK] and it will be inserted in the text.

If incorrect, there are several options. If there is no correct response, check closely to see if one of the responses is substantially correct. If so, it can be selected, introduced into the text and edited. We will show additional ways to correct text later. It often is more efficient to edit an incorrect response than to repeat the [Command]. If none of the responses is usable, re-dictate. The new dictation will also show up in the [Alternates panel]. If correct [OK], and continue dictation.

Editing Words with [Correct] and [Correct that]

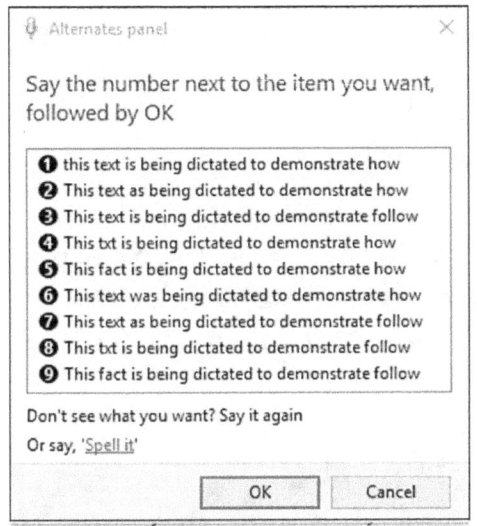

Because of its many functions, this [Command], will often be used instead of [Delete] and [Select], which follows. This is true whether attempting to [Correct] the last phrase, or an individual word, or words. In either case, the selection will be highlighted and the [Alternatives panel] will open.

[Correct] or [Correct that], when not used immediately after dictating, will highlight the letter or word the cursor is "resting against" whether at the beginning, end, or somewhere "inside the word," otherwise, if during current dictation, the [Alternates panel] will open and it will display what was spoken as well as alternates. The [Alternates Panel], as shown, will usually show several potential matches from the database.

Check the results very carefully. Each of them will be numbered. To make corrections say number before the correct word or words. Often the correct response will be number (1). Since it brings up several alternatives you may find that a correct response is not number (1), so check all of them carefully to see if another one is correct.

The correct response may be the second, third, or even the last numbered item. If you get the correct response in any order, identify it by number and OK it. This will place it in the document and you can continue dictating. If all responses are incorrect, speak the phrase again. If unsuccessful, you still have several options. The first, is to speak very clearly, and repeat what was said initially, but not returned. Often this will produce the correct result.

Break It Down

If the phrase is long and has several errors use [Correct that] and try repeating just the first few words of the phrase. If that corrects the first few words accept the change, [OK] it, and continue with the remaining parts of the original phrase or sentence.

To Reverse

To reverse [Correct] or [Correct that] say [Cancel] or [Clear Selection] and the highlighting will be removed. When the selection is unhighlighted the cursor will rest at the end of the last word. You can continue composing from that point forward.

Dictating Difficult Words

After working with Windows Speech Recognition for several years, we appreciate that it "understands" words better when they are in a meaningful context. As we have already mentioned, it has difficulty distinguishing between "'and," "end" and "in; "4," "for," "four," and "fore;" "2," "to," "too," and "two;" and a host of other words, or combination of words, that have similar sounds. Watch for them. They frequently need to be corrected.

Adding words commonly associated with the word that is mistaken will usually produce better results. One successful technique is to place extra words after the target word. You can easily [Delete] (erase) the extra words after the target word. Using this technique, you ensure yourself of more success in receiving the correct "sound alike" word. It also works to include in your dictation words that already appear after the incorrect word or phrase that is already in the text. This also helps the application associate the context. This sounds like additional work, but it often saves re-dictating an entire sentence.

Adding/Deleting Characters

By deletion: often a word will have an "s" at the end, or should have an "s." It is quicker to [Delete] or add the extra "s" than to repeat the word. Other prefixes or endings can be handled in the same way.

Often "ed" can be added simply using [Press] and the characters (ed). The same thing is true with "ly" or "ing." Some of our User's Profiles, for whatever reason, add an unnecessary word, or words, especially during a pause. Be aware when this happens. Generally, it can be remedied by simply [Deleting] them.

If you have difficulty with a word, consider using a word that contains part of the word. For instance, if speech recognition has difficulty with a word like "slick" it can be formed by adding an "s" to lick. We strive for accuracy, but when it is not accomplished, we then shift to expediency.

Let's get the job done with as few additional steps as possible. Remember our primary job is to produce text. Using [Correct] or [Correct that], the corrections will be added to the User's Profile, where they become part of the database.

If you say a phrase and immediately realize that it is not what you wanted to say, you have several options. Use [Delete] and re-dictate. Use [Correct] or [Correct that] and change all or a portion of what was inaccurate.

Use the NATO Alphabet

We have already introduced the [Speech Dictionary]. Words not recognized can be added to the User's Profile using it. Another option is to use [Spell it] which uses the NATO Alphabet. Using this also provides an option to add words to the [speech dictionary]. When the

NATO Quick Guide

NATO ALPHABET ~ SIGNS ~ SYMBOLS

NATO Alphabet / Letter – Code

A as in ALFA
B – BRAVO
C – CHARLIE
D – DELTA
E – ECHO
F – FOXTROT
G – GOLF
H – HOTEL
I – INDIA
J – JULIETT
K – KILO
L – LIMA
M – MIKE
N – NOVEMBER
O – OSCAR
P – PAPA
Q – QUEBEC
R – ROMEO
S – SIERRA
T – TANGO
U – UNIFORM
V – VICTOR
W – WHISKEY
X – XRAY
Y – YANKEE
Z – ZULU

Common Punctuation Marks & Characters.

(.) Period; Dot; Full Stop; Decimal Point
(,) Comma
(:) Colon
(;) Semicolon
(?) Question mark
(') Apostrophe
(!) Exclamation Mark; Exclamation Point
(¶) Paragraph Sign
(+) Plus Sign
(-) Hyphen; Minus Sign; Dash
(=) Equal Sign
(×) Multiplication Sign
(÷) Division Sign

Frequently Used Punctuation Marks & Characters

(") Open/Close Double Quotes
(') Open/Close Single Quote
(*) Asterisk
(@) At Sign
(_) Underscore
(&) Ampersand, And Sign
(/) Forward Slash
(\ ) Backslash
(#) Number Sign
(   ) Open/Close Parentheses
[   ] Open/Close Brackets
{   } Open/Close Brace, Open Curly Bracket
(°) Degree Sign
(§) Section Sign
(>) Greater Than Sign: Open Angle Bracket
(<) Less than Sign: Close Angle Bracket
($) Dollar Sign
(¢) Cent Sign
(£) Pound Sign
(¥) Yen (Japan) Yuan (China)
(¼) One Quarter Sign
(½) One Half Sign
(¾) Three Quarter Sign
(©) Copyright Sign
(®) Registered Sign, Reg. Trademark Sign
(™) Trademark Sign
(~) Tilde (Common in Ebooks)

Less Common Punctuation Marks & Characters

(–) En Dash
(—) Em Dash, Double Dash
(...) Ellipsis; Dot dot dot
(|) Vertical Bar
(//) Double Slash
(`) Back Quote (Bottom Tilde Key)
(«) Open Angle Quote
(») Close Angle Quote

ElCar Publishing December 2017

[Alternates panel] opens use [Spell it]. Consult the NATO Alphabet on the last page. It uses words to represent individual letters of the alphabet. Review the other numerous entries as well.

The [Alternates Panel] will display what looks like a search window. It will have the number 1 above and to the left of the window. This represents the first letter of the word that is being spelled. If the next word began with a "b" the NATO phonic would be "Bravo."

After the first letter is accepted the number 2 will appear to mark the location of the next character. Each successive new letter will occupy the next highest number. Continue using the NATO words until all of the letters of the word are inserted, then use [OK]. To separate words that are not compound words, use a [Space] between them.

After using [OK] the message, "Would you like add this word?" If the answer is yes, √ check the box to record pronunciation after saving changes. This will open the [Speech Dictionary] where the word is pronounced and saved.

[Open Speech Dictionary]

We introduced this in the opening material. If you are having difficulties, producing a word, or you are getting nonsense words, or a consistently misspelled word, use [Open Speech Dictionary]. (Note that the [Command] is [Open Speech Dictionary] and [NOT open THE Speech Dictionary.)

This presents three choices: Add a new word, Prevent a word from being dictated, or Change existing words. This modifies Windows Speech Recognition to individualize the vocabulary.

This is helpful if you notice, usually during a lull in dictation, that some extraneous word, or words, keep popping up on your monitor. If you prevent them from being dictated, they will not appear again. You cannot prevent, however, the dictation of a word that contains a space, number or a symbol.

You can, however, create a substitute word that is similar to one that you have removed so you don't have to continuously spell it. For example "if" kept showing up spontaneously in our documents. We prevented it from appearing. However, when we needed the word we had to use [Spell it]. Instead, we added the word "iffy" as a substitute word. When "if" was needed, we substituted "iffy" and then deleted the last two characters.

To ultimately resolve this, we created a new User's Profile and eliminated the problem.

User's Profile – See Appendix

When [Correct] or [Correct that] is used to edit words the corrections will be added to the User's Profile. This adds words to the database, which increases the accuracy of Speech Recognition. There may be a way to transfer a Users' Profile from one computer to another. See the Appendix. We are using an old application that works for us.

Fourth Bite
[Select/Select that]

Using the [Command] [Select] without [that] does not highlight the last word or phrase that was spoken. It does nothing, or creates the word "select." If using Microsoft Word, it may open a menu called [Select]. When coupled with [that], however, [Select that] operates similar to [Delete that] and [Correct that], in that it selects the last spoken phrase or sentence. Like [Correct that] it highlights it, but the [Alternates Panel] does not open.

4	[Select] [Unselect that]

Think of this as a function which enables the user to hesitate before making a final decision. After it is highlighted, [Delete] or [Correct/Correct that] can be used to make a change. Use the [Command] [Unselect that] or [Clear Selection] to remove the highlighting if no change is made. The cursor will remain after the last character of the last word.

When between words, it will highlight whichever character is nearest to the cursor. If it happens to be between two words with a space on either side of it, it will [Select] the word to the [Left] ← and highlight it. Highlighting, however, will not open the [Alternates Panel].

The question might be asked, "What good is this [Command]?" After [Selecting] a word, it can be used to place the cursor after that word by using [Unselect that]. An additional word can be then inserted after the cursor. Its usefulness becomes more evident, however when used with the (Subcommand) (Word) or (Words), which we will present in the next chapter.

Hesitation (Reminder)

As mentioned earlier, when you hesitate during dictation using [Select that], it will only respond to the last phrase before the hesitation, just like the response of the other Primary Commands we have discussed. Using this [Command] would then highlight only the last spoken phrase. You would then have the same choices as with the other Primary Commands.

Fifth Bite
[Delete] [Correct] and [Select] with (Word) or (Words)

Now that we understand how the first three Primary Commands work, let's examine how they become more functional when coupled with a (Subcommand). Think of these three Primary Commands combined with a (Subcommand) as a dart and dartboard. Consider the specific word or words you have placed in the text as the target word or words. View each set of [Commands] as darts sent to the text to make changes to the target word(s) at a specific place in the document. When the [Command] directs the (Subcommand) to the correct word(s), it performs its function.

We will see how operations are performed by combinations of [Commands] and (Subcommands). The addition of (Subcommands) gives them the ability to target a word or words on the page for deletion, correction, or to be selected for some other purpose.

If you target a single word or words that appear more than once on the page, each word will have either a number in a box or an OK over it. When the requested word appears, select it by either its number or [OK]. The dart is then directed to the designated target word, or words, to make the change.

When [Delete] [Correct] or [Select] with (Subcommands) are directed to a word or words, they receive added flexibility, since they are not limited to modifying words just spoken, or words that the cursor is next to. After reaching the target, they respond as they do when performing their primary function. This adds to the ability to edit words on the fly, when editing a sentence, paragraph or group of paragraphs. [Delete] functions well, when it is directed to delete a specific word or series of words elsewhere in the document.

5	[Delete] [Correct] [Select] Word or Words

EXERCISE CAUTION. Once again, because [Delete] can be used to delete characters, words, phrases, sentences, entire paragraphs, pages, or even entire documents, unless you are absolutely certain something should be deleted, consider using [Select] (# of Units) first. Make certain you want to delete them. You can potentially save much editing by substituting this [Command].

If we want to [Delete] the word "certain" in the last paragraph, the [Command] would be [Delete] (certain). Since it appears twice in that paragraph, numbers or OK would be placed over each instance. Select the one you want deleted and respond with the number or [OK]. The targeted word "certain" would then disappear from that line.

The cursor, however, would remain where it was before the [Command] was given. (Using [Delete] leaves the cursor at the starting point). As we have suggested, [Undo that] usually works to correct [Delete], but don't bet a whole paragraph or a document on it, unless you are willing to lose it. This is a good time to learn to [Save] first.

[Correct]

Using [Correct] the word "certain" would be highlighted in the same way, because it appears several times on this page. When the designated one is selected, the [Alternates Panel] will open. Several options would then be available: The word could be changed from "certain" to "sure," or another word. After the change, or if no change was made, the cursor would remain in front of the word.

[Select]

Using [Select] would also highlight all the words "certain" on the page. They would again be numbered, or have an [OK]. Choose the one you're targeting and either say the number or [OK]. Once selected, it would be highlighted, but it would do nothing else. Unlike using [Delete] or [Correct], the cursor would move to the selected word and it would remain there until another [Command] was given.

If the [Command] [Delete that] were then given, it would be deleted. If the deletion was in error and was restored by using [Undo that], the cursor would remain after the word.

Using [Select] followed by [Unselect that] or [Clear selection] un-highlights the selection and repositions the cursor after the selected word or words. This enables the insertion of additional characters to complete suffixes, or adding additional words to edit the text. The cursor does not return to the starting point.

[Go] [Go to] to a Specific Location
Sixth Bite

The [Commands] [Go] and [Go to] will place the cursor in a specific location. They differ however in what command follows them to position the cursor. See [Commands] 4 and 5 on Page 78. They work similar to the other three Primary Commands, but do not highlight the word or location or in any way change them. They just position

6 More [Go]
[Go to]

the cursor in a pre-determined location.

Under most circumstances, one of the other Primary Commands could be chosen over them, because they also would then perform a specific function at the designated location.

These [Commands], however, present an alternative way to place the cursor at a specific location in the document. Its most noticeable advantage is when one wants to move the cursor a specific number of units usually just a few characters. There are situations where they more efficiently target a specific location, word or the beginning or end of a sentence or paragraph.

Go to (Next/Last /Previous) (# of Units)

Here we will reintroduce another aspect of [Go], which we have already mentioned as part of the first three navigational [Commands]. Remember that [Go] and [Move], while different words, perform the same function.

	Commands/Sub-Commands	
1	[Delete]	(Word)(Next/Last /Previous)(# of Units)
2	[Correct]	(Word)(Next/Last /Previous)(# of Units)
3	[Select]	(Word)(Next/Last/Previous)(# of Units) Word... Word)
4	[Go to] [Move to]	(Word)(Beginning of/ End of) (Next/Previous)(# of Units)
5	[Go] [Move]	(Forward Back)(# of Units) (Before/After)

To simplify, when we use them, we will use [Go], but understand that if [Move] works better for you feel free to use it.

Both [Go] and [Go to] require a (Subcommand) to function. They have no independent action. [Go to] operates like the first three [Commands] with (Word) or (Words). It has the ability to use only a portion of the (Subcommand) (Next/ Last/Previous) (# of Units).

For this [Command], however, it is significant to note that whereas [Last] and [Previous] both work with the other three Primary [Commands], **[Last] does not work with [Go to]**. If for instance you say " [Go to] (last paragraph) if the expression "last paragraph" is in the document, it will reposition the cursor in front it. If not in the document, nothing will happen.

[Go] (Before/After) operates in much the same way as [Select that]. In other words, it also targets a specific word or unit. It only relocates but does not highlight.

[Go to] with other (Subcommands)

We will discuss further actions of [Go to] when used with the other (Subcommands) after we take a break. We first need to take a look at how speech recognition responds to the text.

TIME FOR A BREAK

Before we begin the next bite, let's take a break. We will then discuss the (Subcommand) (Next/Previous) (# of Units). First it is necessary to observe how the application views words, letters, characters, symbols, and punctuation marks.

COUNTING

This is why we took a break. We need to understand how to count words and characters to calculate the (# of Units) we need to position the cursor where we want it, before using all or a portion of the following [Commands] and (Subcommands)

How Do We Count Words?
Seventh Bite

There are different rules for counting words and characters. The

7 Counting Words/ Characters

application counts punctuation marks as words. A period is as much a word as "apricot," or for that matter an "a," "#," or "&." <u>It does NOT count a space as a word.</u> The easiest way to "count" is to count the words first, then the characters, letters, symbols and punctuation. Add everything including the punctuation mark. Remember that. The last sentence contains three "words" not two; because the final period is included in the count. Try this. Question: How many <u>characters</u> are in the phrase "just do it."? Ignore the quotation marks and the question mark.

Counting Characters

When counting characters (or letters) the rules are different. <u>Letters, characters, symbols and spaces are counted</u> as one character. Consider this before deleting or correcting sentences, or portions of a sentence. To do this you need to know how to count characters.

"Just do it." Contains Four Words
How Many Characters?

Use the same example above, "Just do it." As a sentence, it contains four words, because the period is counted as a word. If it contained a (?), it would also be counted as a word.

Now count the <u>characters</u>. Start counting at the beginning or the end of the sentence. First, count the letters in the words. This totals eight. Then count the space between "t" and "d," and continue with the space between "o" and "i." We now have 10. Finally, count the period. We have four words but 11 characters.

-

Where is Your Cursor?

When navigating between characters, or words on a line, the starting point is always the location of the cursor.

If you create your document on a page that measures 5 or 7 inches, wide you would limit the average number of words on each line to 10 to 14 words. You would then need to calculate only 5 to 7 words from either margin to reach a word in the center of the page. If you have wider margins you might have 18 to 20 words per line.

Knowing the average number of words on a line you can to "guesstimate," instead of count. You can guess the number of words to the target, forward or back from the cursor. If you guess incorrectly, you can estimate how many words to move forward or back to find the word you are searching for.

We will see why this is important when we begin the next bite, where we will explore alternate methods of repositioning the cursor. One easy way is using the following applications:

Using [Press] [Ctrl] (h) and [Press] [Ctrl] (f)

Two applications will help locate words in other parts of the document. If using Word 2002 or later [Press] [Ctrl] (h) for Fin<u>d</u> and Re<u>p</u>lace and [G<u>o</u> to] to move to a specific page. In Word 2003 [Press] [Ctrl] (f) for [Find and Replace]. In later editions it is called [Navigation]. For WordPad use (h) for both [Fin<u>d</u>] and [Re<u>p</u>lace].In WordPad [Press] [Ctrl] (f) just for [Fin<u>d</u>].

THE STARTING POINT

Eighth Bite
(Next/Last/Previous)(# of Units)

Remember, when used with any [Command] including (Next/Last/Previous) (# of Units), the movement will always be from the beginning location of the cursor. In counting, it DOES matter if the cursor is at the beginning or the end of the starting word. As already said, [Go to] does not use the (/Last) portion of the [Subcommand]. If used with (Next) as in [Go to] (Next) (five words) starting before the first character of the beginning word it will end after the fifth word. Starting after the last word it will end up after the sixth word.

8 (Next/Last/Previous)
(# of Units)

Remember to count punctuation and symbols when counting by words, but not spaces. Count all characters, including spaces, when

81

counting by characters. Going in the reverse direction the [Command] verbally would be [Go to] (Previous) (five words). If the cursor is after the last character of the last word, after the [Command] is given, the cursor will end up in front of the fifth word.

While [Go to] is functional with only two of the (Subcommands), there are better ways to perform the same action. While in and of itself not particularly useful when compared to other methods, it does help simplify and demonstrate how the first three Primary Commands react to the (Subcommand) (Next/Previous).

If we understand how the applicable portions of (Subcommands) work with [Go to] we can accurately predict how they will also respond when used with the three Primary Commands.

[Delete]

It is easy to visualize how [Delete] would respond if used with any of the above (Subcommands). If used with (Next/Last/Previous) (# of) words, sentences, or paragraphs you can expect they would be deleted. If the [Command] was given in error or it was later decided not to [Delete] the selection [Undo that] would under most circumstances restore the original word or words.

[Correct] or [Select]

Using either [Correct] or [Select] with (Next) (five words) the cursor would land in the same place. The selected words would be highlighted. With [Correct] the [Alternates panel] would open; whereas, with [Select] the words would remain highlighted, but it would not open. With [Correct], if it were determined that no changes were to be made, use [Cancel]. The [Alternates panel] would close, and the words or words would become un-highlighted.

With [Select] either [Unselect] or [Clear Selection] would clear the highlighting. One would have the option of using either [Delete], or [Correct] or simply un-highlighting using [Clear Selection] to place the cursor after the last selected word.

After highlighting more than one paragraph, [Clear Selection] will leave the cursor at the end of the last paragraph. On the other hand, if the [Command] is [Press] (Home) the cursor will move to the beginning of the first paragraph. On a single paragraph Use [Unselect] to be at the end of the paragraph(s). [Home] to be at the beginning.

If more than a couple of paragraphs are selected often the highlighting is messed up, and it will not be cleared with any [Command]. To clear, turn Speech Recognition [Off]. Manually go down to the bottom of the last paragraph plant the cursor and [Enter].

While we have covered much so far, there are still several important [Commands] and (Subcommands) we need to consider to make navigation even more precise.,

More [Go] and Additional Commands

When you do a lot of composing, you will find that additional [Commands] are more helpful because they present alternatives. When the first choice does not give the expected result, do not hesitate to use an alternative.

	Commands/Sub-Commands	
1	[Delete]	(Word)(Next/Last / Previous)(# of Units)
2	[Correct]	(Word)(Next/Last / Previous)(# of Units)
3	[Select]	(Word)(Next/Last/ Previous)(# of Units) Word... Word)
4	[Go to] [Move to]	(Word)(Beginning of/ End of) (Next/Previous)(# of Units)
5	[Go] [Move]	(Forward Back)(# of Units) (Before/After)

[Go to], like the three [Commands] before it, can also be directed to a word or words or a phrase and with the addition of (Beginning of/End of) it targets the beginning or end of a sentence, paragraph or the document. You can also use (Start of) Document) and [End of] document.

We have found the best success in using these [Commands] is to emphasize (**OF**) in the [Command]; [Go to] (Beginning **OF**/End **OF**) (sentence, paragraph, etc.) Another alternative is to create a macro, to change the [Command]. We will discuss this later.

[Go to] Pinpoint a Location

When [Go to] targets a Word or Words, it puts the cursor before the target word(s). When [Go] is used with (Before/After) it can place the cursor either before or after a word or words. [Go](Forward/ Back) (# of Units) works in the same way. These [Commands] are particularly helpful when making small changes such as deleting or adding another character, deleting or adding another character in the middle of a word or adding an ending to a word.

It has many other uses including separating a word that is normally two separate words. This is helpful also when moving forward or back one, two or three characters or words, to position the cursor so it can respond to another [Command] that will complete the necessary change. It can also be used with sentences and paragraphs.

This is important, because some tools seem to work better to accomplish a task than others. We have generally found [Go] (After) a specific word or set of words works better for us than using (Before). But another user might find the opposite to be true.

Experiment with the [Go] and [Go to] Commands.

Review and practice with all of the (Subcommands) that go with [Go to] and [Go]. While they duplicate what other (Subcommands) can do the user will encounter situations where they will be helpful

[Select] (Word... Word)

This is the last combination of [Commands] that constitute the "Magic" of Windows Speech Recognition. To give this [Command], first [Select] and then target a word in a phrase or sentence to [Copy], [Delete], or [Correct], and follow it with the last word in that group of words.For instance, if we wished to [Select] "phrase" through "word" in the last sentence, the [Command] would be [Select] (phrase through word). [Select] will highlight the selection, but unlike [Correct] it will not open up the [Alternates panel]. This has multiple uses. It can be used to select an entire phrase, and is particularly helpful when [Deleting] or [Copying] a phrase or series of words, to use again elsewhere. It is an alternative to the other three Primary Commands and serves a function much like [Select], [Correct] or [Delete] with the (Next/Last/Previous) (#of Units).

The same thing can be accomplished, of course, by going to the beginning word with [Select] followed by (Next) (16 words). This produces the same result. So use either (Word…Word) or [Select] followed by the number of words.

Microsoft Speech Recognition Tutorials

If you cut corners and have not completed all of the Microsoft Tutorials, now is the time to finish them to improve your success with Windows Speech Recognition.

~CHAPTER EIGHT~

THE RABBIT IS OUT OF THE HAT

We have now completed the most challenging, and also the most productive components of Windows Speech Recognition. The ability to create text and navigate within a document to make necessary changes or corrections without using the keyboard or mouse is the hallmark of any speech recognition application.

Another feature of Windows Speech Recognition is the ability to execute many of the [Commands] necessary to format a document. After learning Windows Speech Recognition it will be used on various projects and will require formatting the word editors and processors used with speech recognition. Accordingly, again using WordPad as an example and some features of Microsoft Word will be reviewed. Some are as easily selected using just the cursor.

FORMATTING YOUR WORD EDITOR/PROCESSOR

Additional [Commands] for Formatting Documents

Menus in Notepad

A good example of menus is Windows Notepad, which contains five main menu items [File] [Edit] [Format] [View] and [Help]. We have expanded these to show sub-menus. Become familiar with these.

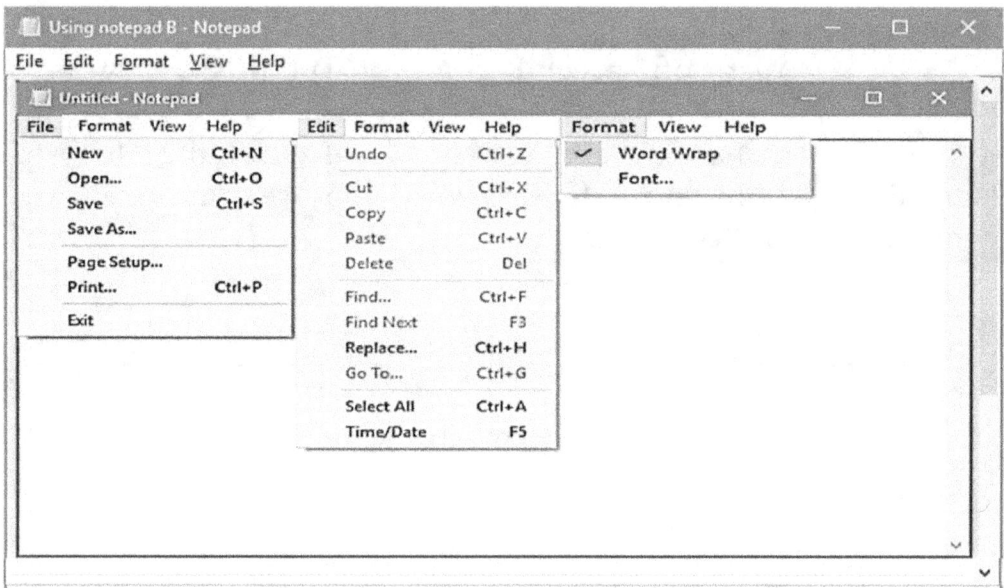

Menu items were expanded with WordPad/Windows 7 and Word 2007, with the addition of the Ribbon. While showing only three main

menus [File], [Home], and [View], the Ribbon shows both the main and sub-menus of each menu. A format similar to the [Home] menu appears on the other two menus, [File] and [View]. The addition of the Ribbon entries above or below the Menu items enables positioning them for easy viewing outside the main Menus.

Any of the items on the Ribbon can also be shifted to the Quick Access Toolbar, which can be placed either above or below the main menus. Most people would prefer to have them above.

They are added to the Ribbon by a [Left] click on the symbol above the File Menus, which we circled in the image to the [Left]. When clicked, a window will show the message [Customize Quick Access Toolbar]. Before establishing the order of the menu items which will appear, carefully plan it to avoid the unnecessary challenge of having to change it later. To access the same on Microsoft Word use [File] [Options] [Customize Ribbon].

The ribbon can be minimized during composing by clicking on the small (^) to the right of the (?) on WordPad. For Word on the [Home] menu click on the screen with an up arrow in upper [Right] hand corner next to the (?) mark.

WordPad/Windows 10 with Ribbon Minimized

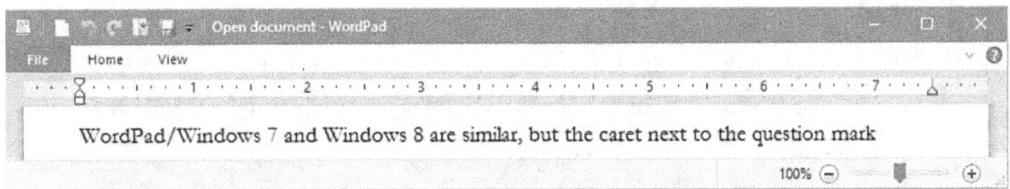

The menu and the items on the Quick Access Toolbar are readily available when minimized. To return to the Ribbon click on the same symbol as described above.

Table 2 Column A, which follows, summarizes the formatting elements of WordPad. [Finish] reminds users of WordPad who have created text with speech recognition can [Past] their content to OpenOffice or LibreOffice which enables formatting, mirror images and the ability to create PDF files.

Table 2 Column A and B

Table 2 Column A			~ Table 2 Column B		
Command	Detail	Misc	Other FREE Writer's Tool Kit Items		
Review Quick-Guides	Copies of Quick-Guides in Appendix	Learn how Practice, Practice,	Speech Recognition Macros	Customize WSR Commands	Download Templates From Net
Microsoft WordPad/Word Formatting	[File][Home] [View] [Keys] Shortcuts	[Press][Alt] (F)(H)(V) Shortcuts	Navigation [Switch] to [Desktop]	[Switch Applications]	From Desktop to Applications
[Page Setup] [Margins] [Save][Print]	[File] (Sub – Commands)	Location Varies with Application	Create Tables/ Convert Images	Appearance/ Publication	Presentation of Data
Zoom - Ruler Word Wrap	[View] Set Ruler and Word Wrap	Ruler Formats Text to Screen	PDF Editors PDF Viewers Ultrafilesearch	Convert Files and Images Search	Create Image Produce Text Find Files
Finish WordPad with OpenOffice	Speech Recognition WordPad	[Paste] Format in OpenOffice	Paint.NET	Image Editors Snipping Tool	Convert Image for Document
Lines Paragraphs Alignment	[Home] Spacing Left, Right, Justify	[Press] [Ctrl] [L] [R] [J] [E/Center]	OCR Scrivener yWriter	Recovery Novels and Projects	Digital Text For Writers and Research
Expand Collapse Ribbon	[Home] Increase Text Area	Increase/ Decrease Menu Items	Text-to-Speech Sound Editors	Free and Commercial Applications	TypeIt Readit 3 Commercial Applications
[Text] [Font] [Text Color]	[Home] Size Color of fonts Background	Text/Font Term Varies by App	MultiPurpose Caliibre	Library Mgr. e-books	Novelists Detailed Compositions
Bold](B) Underline](U) [Italicize] (I)	Change Appearance of Font	[Press] [Ctrl] (B) (U) (I) Repeat	Self-Motivated Author	Self-Publishing I Ought to Write a Book	Paperback KDP- Smash-words e-Books
[Caps/No Cap/ Lower Case Headings	Caps No Caps Modified Headings	[Press] [Ctrl] (E)(L)(R)(J)	Create Your Own Website	Free Website and Domain	Weebly and Others
[Insert] Picture/ Draw	WordPad Check out Draw	[Word] [Insert] Application	Self-editing Revision and Proofreading	Free Online Resources Commercial	Slickwrite Hemingway Grammarly
[Copy][Paste] Vs [Cut] [Paste]	Note Page # [Copy][Paste] Return [Cut]	Copy data Move/ Paste Return/Delete	Commercial Editors	Serenity Editor Grammarly	For the Serious Prolific Writer
[Press][Ctrl] (f) (h)	Find and Replace	Search/Find/ Replace	Free Internet Resources Viristotal	Tech Tools And Otherss File check	Resources on Line
Enable Dictation Scratchpad	Extend Use of Speech Recognition	Other Apps Other than Microsoft	Quick-Guides Tables 1 & 2 Other Guides	Miscellaneous Helps Wrap up	Additional Information on Subjects

ElCar Publishing August 2018

Experiment with [Show Numbers] and [Mouse Grid] on Internet!

We continue with a discussion of additional menu items summarized on Table 2 Column A and B which begins with a reminder to consult the Quick Guides we have presented. Familiarize yourself with the file structure of WordPad, Word, or your word editor.

[File] Page Setup

This and the following features are on the menus of WordPad. They apply directly to WordPad, but all word editors and word processors have similar features. If using another word editor or word processor find the applicable menu item to accomplish the same thing.

When setting up any word processor it is necessary to define the parameters of the page. To begin a new document with WordPad open [File] and [Page Setup]. Set the page size; determine the orientation (portrait or landscape); set the margins (in inches) and set whether the pages will be numbered when printed. In addition to standard letter size, there are some 21 other sizes. Not all the others, however, show the dimensions in inches.

[File] Page Setup Margins

Using Letter size, begin by setting the [Left] margin. This defaults to

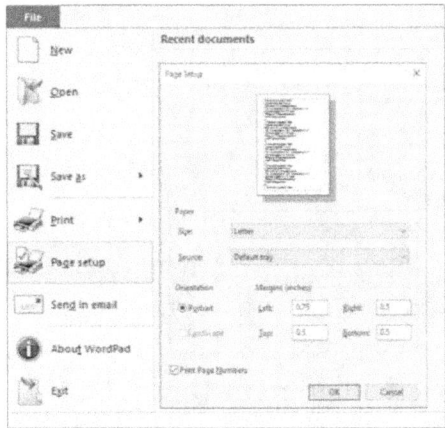

1.25, but choose margins that complement the size appropriate for your project. The numerals can be spoken, or set manually.

Use [TAB] to enter the next field. Entering them manually is quicker because the program does not always like to translate 0.5, 0.75, or other decimals by voice.

Here you can also designate whether to have page numbers printed. [New], [Save], [Print] as well as [Page Setup] are found under the [File] menu. The next couple of items are under the [View] menu.

89

[View] Window Word Wrap

Check the [Ruler] and [Word Wrap]. We set the word wrap to [Wrap to window] but it can be set to [Wrap to ruler]. If set to [No wrap] text will be produced in one long, long continuous line reaching out to infinity.

These [Commands] are behind the [View] menu if you have not 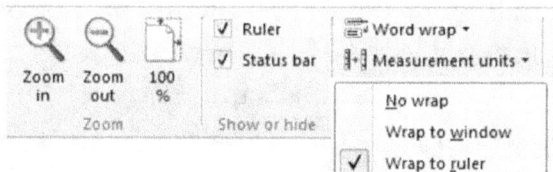 moved them to the Quick Access Toolbar. The two magnifying glasses increase or reduce the size of the view shown on the page. Checking the status bar will produce a bar at the bottom of the page, which will change the size of the viewing area.

[Home] Paragraphs/Line Spacing

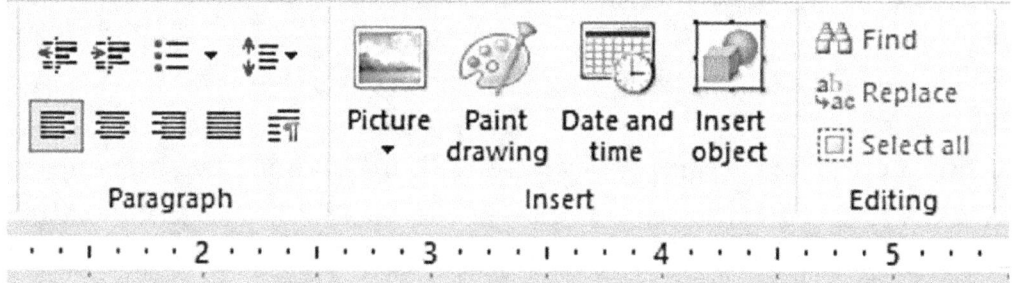

Paragraph

In the second row of [Paragraph], the 5th series of lines containing the ¶ (Pilcrow) offers choices for [Line Spacing] 1.0 through 2. Do not use the option of adding 10-point spacing after paragraphs.

This is also where you set up the paragraph alignment [Left], [Right], [Center], or [Justified]. The menu immediately above it is [Line Spacing], which duplicates what we have already seen. Remember WordPad does not allow [Mirror Images]. These are necessary if producing a book because of the spine. If using only WordPad, to create a book [Paste] the results into OpenOffice or LibreOffice. See page 96. Microsoft Online will [Copy] [Mirror Images] but will not create them.

[Home] Expand Collapse Ribbon

Ribbons are helpful, but they occupy space. They can be collapsed by locating the caret (^) to the [Left] of the circled (?) in the upper Right] corner of the Ribbon on WordPad/Window 7 and current. The Ribbon is collapsed on Word by clicking on the Ribbon Display Option, this time to the [Right] of the (?) in the upper [Right] corner.

Other Options

Fonts are selected on the [Home] menu. It is located under, but is not part of the [View] menu Default is Calibri 11.

[Home] (Font)

Fonts and size are selected here. These are best selected manually, but they can be set by voice. To the [Right] of that are two Aa's. They increase/decrease the viewing size of the text.

[Text Color] (Font Color) [Highlight]

For WordPad the [Command] is [Text Color]. It is to the [Left] of the five paragraph images on the WordPad Ribbon. This is below the 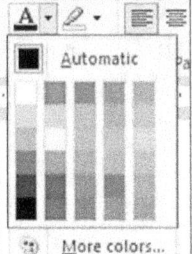 double A's. For other applications, it is called [Font Color]. Select Automatic for black. This tutorial is printed in black and white. If it were in color, you could see one of 30 different colors.

The [Highlight] pencil is found to the [Right] of [Text Color] with 15 choices. When the cursor goes over the color blocks, the color of the blocks will be identified by name. The selected color will then appear in your document. The [Text Color] will continue to be the color of your document until you change it to another color, or back to black.

Change Back to Black

Change the Text color back to "Black" or "Automatic" when you resume. Enter a space after the last colored character and again give the [Command] [Text Color]. Select black, or simply say, "black."

[Bold] [Italic] [Underline] [Unselect]

These appear under the name of the font. Some other specialized functions are there as well. These functions also have alternatives.

Saying just the words [Bold], [Italics], [Underline] and [Unselect] 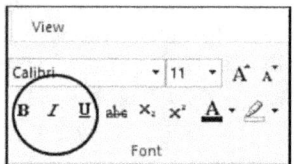 usually work. If they do not, there are alternatives. To choose any of them you must first [Select] what you want to highlight, then choose the new appearance. Then these can also be performed by speech recognition using the [Commands] listed below, beginning with [Press].

    [Bold] = [Press] [Ctrl] (B)
    [Italicize] = [Press] [Ctrl] (I)
    [Underline] = [Press] [Ctrl] (U)
    [Insert] (Picture/Paint Drawing)

[Caps / No Caps/Lowercase]

We touched on this earlier. To capitalize an individual character, use [Go] (Before/After), place the cursor before (or after) the character to be capitalized [Select] (Next/Last) (#Units) and [Cap that].

If it is already capitalized in error, use the same procedure, but instead use the [Command] [Lowercase that] Use the same procedure to capitalize or lowercase a word, phrase, sentence, or paragraph.

[Insert] and [Editing]

Word Wrap works for text in WordPad. [Images] can be [Inserted], but the text will not wrap around them. [Insert] pictures, but remember they may need to be [Inserted] again if the manuscript is re-formatted in a word processor. The other items on this end of the Ribbon, except for Paint Drawings, are self-explanatory. If using WordPad explore the paint-drawing feature. This will be of interest to both adults and children.

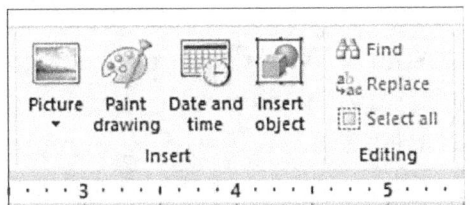

[Copy][Paste][Cut]

These familiar [Commands] are also found on the [Home] menu, where they would be expected. You will first, again, use the [Command] [Select], or manually designate the words, sentences or paragraphs you wish to [Copy], [Paste] or [Cut]. With either [Delete] or [Cut] you can [Paste] what was selected in another location. If you use [Undo], it will simply replace the data in the same location.

As indicated previously, before [Copying] or [Cutting] and [Pasting] in most instances we recommend [Copying] instead of [Cutting]. We do this if it is an important or complex section because we do not want to take a chance that somehow the data will be lost. When successful you can [Delete] it from the original location.

[Press] [Ctrl] (f) and (h)

Use [Ctrl] (f) to find a word. Use [Ctrl] (h) if you want to replace a word. These are helpful when you find that you have used a word incorrectly several times. Place the wrong word in the first box, the correct one in the second. Scroll through all instances of the suspected incorrect word and then correct only those where it is wrong.

Changing all of them you might inadvertently change one that has been properly used. (These will differ in some of the Microsoft Word processors). [Ctrl] (h) is also used to go to a specific page. This is particularly helpful during the editing process.

Setting Page Sizes for Books

If you do not have a compatible Microsoft Word processing application and are using WordPad to compose (dictate) pages for a standard size trade book, you will find that the page sizes given are not the standard trade sizes of 5.25x 8, 6 x 9, or 6.69x.9.61 which is the original size of this book, or other standard sizes.

Solution – ISO Paper Sizes?

An apparent solution to this problem would be to search the Internet for a web site which gives International Paper sizes, such as found at **ISO Paper Sizes | Still Creek Press**, and choose the International Paper size closest to the paper size given in WordPad. Example A5 = 5.83 x 8.27 inches which is as close as you can get for a 6 x9 book. You could compromise and set the page size in WordPad at A5.

A Better Solution – OpenOffice or LibreOffice

A better solution, however, is to avoid this problem entirely by using a free word processor where standard pages can be created. Since you also need other features that are not part of WordPad, such as Mirror Images, and the ability to create PDF files, a solution is to [Open] OpenOffice or LibreOffice and [Paste] text produced by WordPad.

Text can be created with WordPad using Windows Speech Recognition, and when [Pasted] into them for formatting in a form that will enable you to self-publish a book, if have such an inclination.

USING WORDPAD AND OPENOFFICE TOGETHER

If you do not have or use any compatible Microsoft Word processors to create and finish your documents, you can use Microsoft WordPad with Windows Speech Recognition to compose text. This can be [Copied] and [Pasted] into OpenOffice or LibreOffice, free word processors, both of which have both "Mirror Images" and can produce PDF files.

How We Set the Margins for OpenOffice

To determine comparable margin settings for OpenOffice, we copied a 6 x9 page from another book that is being edited and [Pasted] it into OpenOffice, which does not have a setting for the gutter (spine). We compensated for this by first setting the margins at 0.50 for all margins in Word 2013 including the gutter. Using this as a base we made necessary changes on OpenOffice margins.

We can emulate the formatting of Microsoft Word 2013 6 x 9, using Garamond 14 fonts, by setting the OpenOffice Inner Margin at 0.90, Outer at 0.50, Top at .50 and Bottom at 0.30. To Set Page numbers, use [Insert] then [Footer] and then [Insert] [Fields] [Page number] into the Footer and [Center]. This will approximate the same number lines per page, in the initial view, but may print out one line less. Experiment with this.

For PDF files, Open OpenOffice [Print] [Export as PDF]. Use [Lossless compression], [Reduce Image resolution] set as [300 DPI], Select under [General PDF/A-1a] and [Embed this document inside the PDF]. Set margins in OpenOffice as we described above. Experiment with these settings, also, but they worked well for us.

Settings for WordPad

To set up WordPad to approximate the same view use the following procedure. Under [File] [Page setup], set WordPad page at Letter 8.5"x11" portrait orientation. Set all margins at 0.5. Set Word wrap to window. Line Spacing 1.00. Use the same font as used in OpenOffice. Open WordPad. [Copy] and [Paste] a full OpenOffice document into WordPad. Adjust the WordPad view to help visualize your work.

Adjusting WordPad

There are three symbols in the upper [Right] hand corner of the application. They are from left to right [-] [□] and [X]. Click on the [□] which will enable changing the size of the screen. Using the cursor place it on the [Right] margin and pull it towards the center until the text approximates the appearance of the text on the [Right] hand margin of the OpenOffice document as shown below.

OpenOffice and WordPad

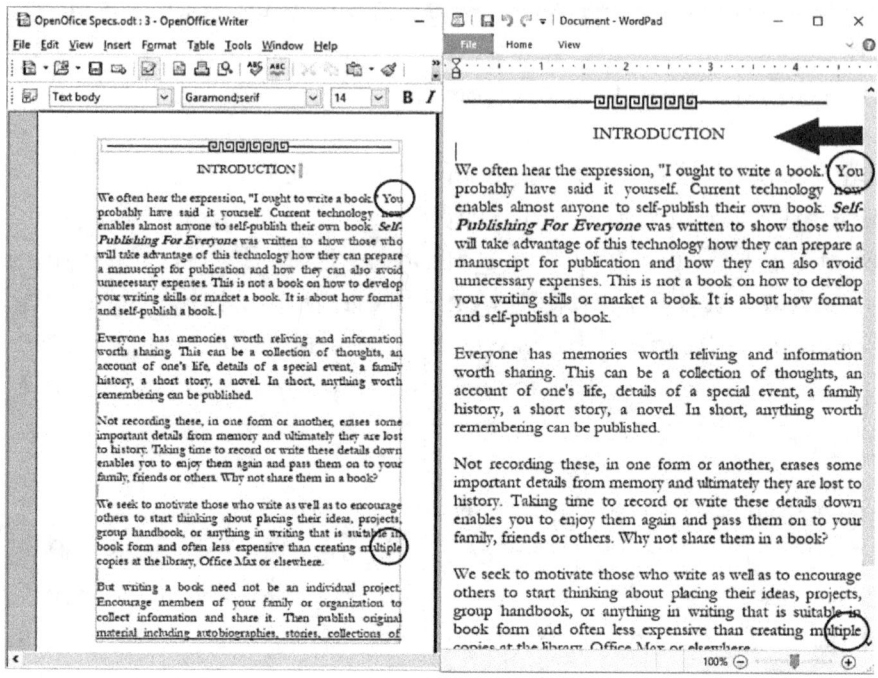

To Make it More Accurate

On this page the WordPad document is shown on the [Right], OpenOffice on the [Left]. To reasonably duplicate the appearance of the OpenOffice document view, use the same font and check the last character on every line in WordPad against the corresponding character in OpenOffice. Adjust the WordPad margin to create these settings when you prepare your document. It will require experimentation. Adjust settings for other book sizes.

LibreOffice

For LibreOffice use the same settings. To set page number however first use [Insert] [Header and Footer] (Footer) then [Insert] (Page Number) (1) and [Center]. Adjust as necessary for other book sizes.

~CHAPTER NINE~
Enable Dictation Scratchpad
In Various Applications

Enable Dictation Scratchpad in Excel Spreadsheets

We mentioned this application in Chapter Three on page 31 because occasionally it will activate without prompting. As we explained there, however, this application was designed to introduce text into applications that do not allow text to be introduced directly with Microsoft Windows Speech Recognition.

Not everyone using Windows Speech Recognition will have a Microsoft Word application compatible with it. For those using WordPad, text created with it can be [Copied] and [Pasted] into OpenOffice or LibreOffice, earlier editions of Microsoft Word and [Enable dictation scratchpad] would therefore not be necessary.

We will refer to this application as [Scratchpad]. We have found it can be helpful in composing text and data into Microsoft Excel spreadsheets. We have experimented but have not found any non-Microsoft spreadsheets that allows its use.

We first experimented with Excel 2010 which is part of Microsoft Office 2010. It works well with that edition. When we first tested it, dictation was first entered into [Scratchpad] and then [Inserted] into the spreadsheet. The procedure was as follows:

Using [Enable dictation scratchpad]

See the image on the next page. We first used the curser by grasping the line between Column A and Column B to expand Column A. We then highlighted Columns B and C. By [Right] clicking on the highlighted area and then [Left] clicking on [Format Cells] we chose [Currency], the $ sign and two decimal points. All numbers placed in those columns would therefore be displayed in dollars and cents.

Excel 2010

	A	B	C	D
1	Business Expenses	Unit One	Unit Two	
2				
3				
4	Automobile Expenses	$225.00		
5	Freight Expenses	$225.00	$200.00	
6	Equipment Rental	$282.59	$2,010.12	
7	Advertising Expense	$592.75	$20,010.00	
8	Rental Expense	$695.12		
9	Experimentation expense lab	$12.50	$200.	
10	Printing Expense	$497.20		

(Cell A10 selected, formula bar shows "Printing Expense". A dialog shows "Printing expense" with Insert and Cancel buttons.)

We then created the Headings on Line 1 cells A-C. Beginning with Column A on the [Left], we entered the data, instead of using [Insert] we used [Press] (Right Arrow). This moved the cursor to Cell B. Entering the Heading, it was also used to go to Cell C.

When we completed Cell C we used [Insert] and the cursor moved down one line to line 2. [Insert] moves the cursor down one cell. We used [Insert] (twice) to get to line four. To get back Column A on line 4 we used [Press] (Left Arrow) (twice). This placed the cursor so we could enter the Description on line 4 (Automobile Expenses).

After entering Automobile Expense we moved the cursor to Column B (Unit One), again using [Press], but this time (Right Arrow). We then composed the number 225 which appeared as $225.00. There were no figures for Unit Two so no entries were necessary. Using [Enter] the cursor dropped to line 5.

Using [Press] (Left Arrow) we then entered Column A again, where we entered Freight Expenses. With [Press] (Right Arrow) we entered and completed the Unit One expense of $225.00. Again, with [Press] (Right Arrow) we entered and completed the Unit Two entry of $200.00. Using [Enter] followed by [Press] (Left Arrow) (twice) we returned to column A. The rest of the spreadsheet was completed using the same [Commands] in the same way.

When using [Enable dictation scratchpad] any changes need to be made in the scratchpad. It operates by the [Commands] used for other speech recognition compositions. All information can be removed by using [Select] (all) and [Delete]. Individual characters or numbers can be located using [Go] (Back) (# Units).

Totaling Columns

For the uninitiated, cells are added in Excel using the formula [=Sum (A1:A24)] and [Enter]. In this example the first column would be A1 and the last A24. No spaces just =SUM(A1:A24).

Direct Entry

When we rechecked our initial spreadsheet with Excel 2013 and also with Microsoft Excel Online we discovered that entries in these editions are not first placed in [Scratchpad] and then transferred to the spreadsheet. They were entered directly. The entries in the scratchpad had to be exact because they could not be corrected by voice after entered.

Excel Mobile

We have experimented with Excel Mobile with three Tablets. The largest one is a 10.1 inch. All three of them qualify for and have Microsoft Excel Mobile. (As well as Microsoft Word Mobile).

We thought we would be using [Enable dictation scratchpad] to enter data into the Excel spreadsheet. We found, however, that the data was not entered in the [Scratchpad] either.

Instead, it was entered directly in the space above the column and also in the correct cell.

Dictating into Excel Mobile

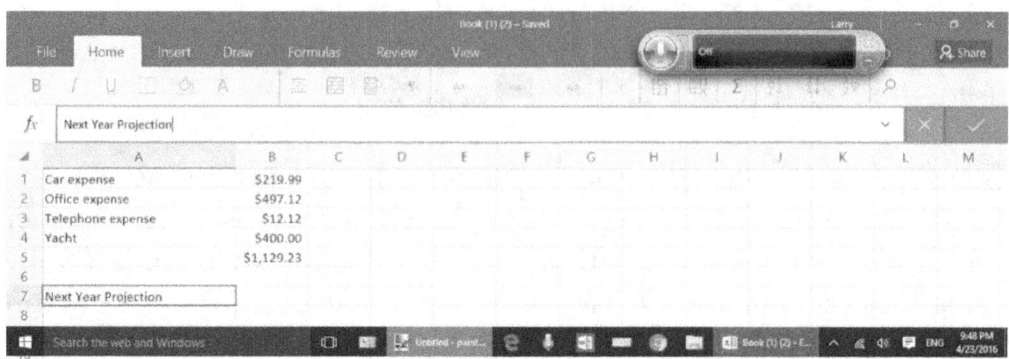

Practical Application

On a recent project we used speech recognition and had approximately 90% accuracy. The key is to dictate normally such as (three hundred twenty five dollars eight cents) because they are placed in formatted columns they will appear as currency. On that project, of perhaps 25 entries, most dictated dollar amounts were correct.

"2's" created the most problem. But if not the first number they usually did not. Remember when using [Scratchpad], in Microsoft Excel, or any application that permits it, all corrections need to be made in the text box. Use [Press] and the number(s) if necessary. After the data is correct, use [Insert] to place it in a cell. Changes cannot be made by voice after data has been inserted into the spreadsheet.

It was still quicker for us, to compose the subject lines and the dollar amounts, than typing them in. This was particularly true when using a laptop. Desktops set up with the keyboard shelf make it easier to type data. Our experiment was to determine if using [Scratchpad] was a reasonable alternative to typing. Results? Possible, but practical?

Not Uniform Results

Because of differences in applications, computers, and users, we can not always anticipate getting the same result when following a set procedure. If this occurs strive to find an alternative to accomplish the same goal. Accuracy is as important as speed.

Other Applications

This application also works with some non-Microsoft applications. Experiment with some of your favorites that do not permit the dictation of text directly using Windows Speech Recognition.

Other Uses for Enable Dictation Scratchpad

[Scratchpad] also activates when searching the Internet with speech recognition. If there is already data in the search box place the cursor in the search box and use [Ctrl] and (a), which will highlight it and then use [Delete] to clear it. Then dictate the request. It will first appear in the [Scratchpad] [Text box]. If correct, [Insert] and [Enter]. When the menu opens use [Mouse Grid]. Zero in on the best match and [Double Click].

Cortana

Using Microsoft Windows 10, we have Cortana to help with searching. She will also do a good job locating your request. If modifying the search with Windows Speech Recognition, you can pick the best result by using [Mouse Grid] and [Double click] it.

Google Now

If using Google Chrome, you have the option of using [Google Now] 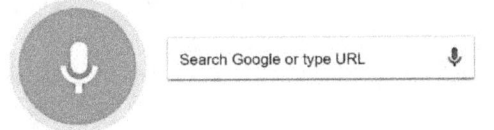 to search. In the composite image, it is first a microphone symbol at the [Right] end of a search box. This is shown in the image as the Microphone, [Click] on it. When it says "Speak now," it shows a large twice-circled microphone on the [Left] symbol which shows "Listening." Say your request.

~ CHAPTER TEN ~
Macros
For
Windows Speech Recognition

We have discussed Mini-Macros, which can be created with [Open Speech Dictionary]. Windows Speech Recognition Macros expands on what can be created and placed in compatible word editors or processors with voice-activated macros, to perform repetitive tasks, and enable speech control over some functions of a computer.

Definition

First, let's define "macro." A search provides this simple definition under the subject of macros as used with computers:

> A single instruction that expands automatically into a set of instructions to perform a particular task.

When we created a Quick Guide for Alternate Commands, we repeatedly used the expressions [Press] [Alt] and [Press] [Ctrl]. Rather than typing the phrases, we created two macros [Press] [Alt] and [Press] [Ctrl]. These created the word and characters without having to repeat the words and characters each time they were used.

We automated the task by creating these Macros. This is what a macro is designed to do.

Macros were introduced as an application in Microsoft Vista. It continues to be available in Windows 7, Windows 8 and Windows 10.

Like Windows Speech Recognition, this also at first appears to be a well-kept secret.

A Little Complicated – But Worth It!

For many, this process will seem too complicated. But if Windows Speech Recognition is frequently used, especially with unusual phrases or formulas, it will prove worthwhile. Following are simplified instructions on how to download and use this application:

Preview of Steps

1. Download Windows Speech Recognition Macros. The current site is below. Websites frequently change. If it is not there, search for it by name. Download both the application and the Release Notes. Review the release notes before starting.

https://www.microsoft.com/en-s/download/details.aspx?id=13045

The Task Bar

2. For Windows Vista and Windows 7: locate the macro with [Start] [All Programs], create a shortcut and pin [Windows Speech Recognition Macros] to the taskbar and run it. 2b. For Windows 8 and Windows do the same.

3. On the taskbar, [Right] click on the Macro icon. Then [Left] click on [Windows Speech Recognition Macros] when it appears on the taskbar. This is the first circle on the taskbar above. This will activate the Windows Speech Recognition application. Here is where it gets interesting. Next, locate the pyramid symbol (▲) on the taskbar or a (^) carat symbol on the Windows 10 taskbar. In the image above, this shows a flag. On the Windows 10 operating system it shows the carat. [Left] click on which appears.

4. The Windows Speech Recognition Macro image appears as a very tiny replica of the Windows Speech Recognition Macros symbol. Use the cursor to move over the items in this menu if you have difficulty seeing it. When it is identified [Right] click on it. The bottom of that menu may or may not show [Customize ...]

Composite Image

5. The [New Speech Macro ...] will appear at the center in the image below. Place the cursor on [Security] in the center block. It will open

Windows Speech Recognition Macros

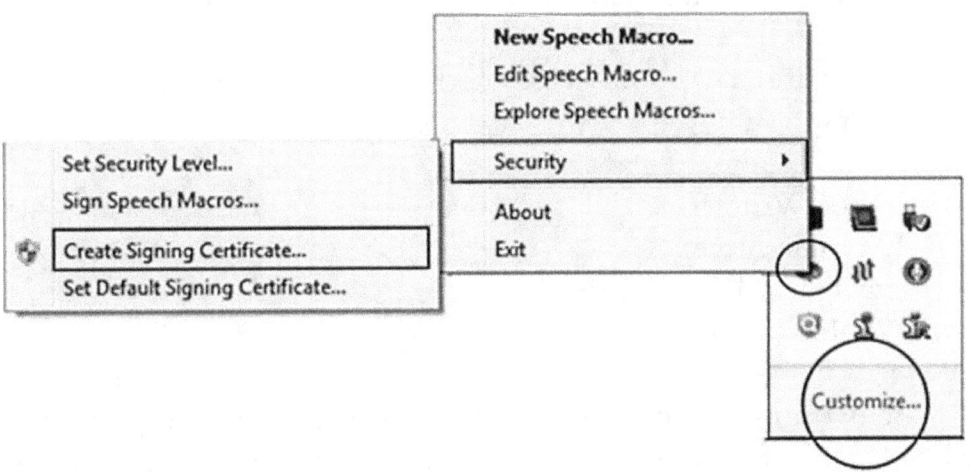

the menu to the left. [Left] click on [Create Signing Certificate]. Set Security Level. Choose between High and Medium [OK]. [Certificate Created] will appear, [OK] it.

6. Go back to step 5. This time use [New Speech Macro...]. You are now ready to begin creating a macro. Select [New Speech Macro... [Insert Text].

7. Create a macro. Place "Address Example" in the first address line. (Do not include the quotation marks.) And in the second line we will begin the macro, which in this case is an address complete with zip code and telephone number.

Bubba Writer
123 Main Street
AnyTown, USA 12345
123-456-7890

Note the box before ☐ Digitally sign this Speech Macro, √ check this which is (Recommended). Since you have already created a certificate this should be checked. Proceed to [Create].

[Next]. A [New Speech Macro] window will appear providing a summary. [Signing data with your private signature key] window will open. [OK] [Windows Speech Recognition Macros] window will open showing [New Speech Macro] created [Close].

Open a compatible word processor and say, "Address Example," with the following result:

Bubba Writer
123 Main Street
AnyTown, USA 12345
123-456-7890

8. Create two more macros. Entitle the first [Bracket Right] (without the brackets) in the Enter text portion type [Right], with the brackets, be sure to capitalize it. Complete that and then create another [Bracket Left] without brackets, [Left] in the bottom half. The first will contain the word [Right] with brackets around it. The second [Left] with brackets around it. You can use any words or symbols. This is just an example to show what it can be done.

Summary

If you did not get the expected results, read the instructions again and try again. You need to create [Signing Certificate] and digitally sign each macro. When used often this will become a habit.

Emulate Commands

It is sometimes difficult for speech recognition to recognize [Go to] (Beginning/End) of (Sentence), (Paragraph) of (Document). It has been suggested by someone to replace those [Commands] to the top and bottom of the document with [Top] and [Bottom] macros. We have frequently had difficulty with these [Commands] and have used those suggestions. We will use them in examples on how the [Emulate Recognition] works for this operation.

Create Macro with Emulate Recognition

1. Open [New Speech Macro].
2. [Emulate Recognition].
3. In the first portion insert [Beginning] (without the brackets).
4. In the main portion insert [Go to the beginning of document], again without the brackets.
5. [Next] [Create] [New Speech Macro], which will appear, check "Digitally Sign this Speech Macro (Recommended)."
6. [Create] [Windows Speech Recognition Macros] window will open showing New Speech Macro created [Close]. The word "Beginning" can be used instead of [Go to the beginning of document].
7. Test in an open word editor or processor, unless you are already at the top, or bottom, of a document.

Create Second Macro with Emulate Recognition

Use the same procedure to create the alternate macro, which will bring you to the bottom of a document. It will be entitled [Bottom] on first line and [Go to end of document] in the main body. Complete as above. Test both Macros.

Create New Alternatives with Emulate Recognition

If the user has difficulty with a specific [Command] they can create an alternative [Command] with the [Emulate Recognition] option. For the imaginative, this application has almost in-exhaustible possibilities. Note: if you create "gag" macros, make sure they don't pop up in your regular dictation – they might be embarrassing. (See under [Advanced] Menu Macros).

Macros Deactivate on Shutdown

When the computer is [Shut Down] all macros that have been created will be [Saved], but they will not be active again until they are reset by using [Set Default Signing Certificate] or [Create Signing Certificate] and [Sign Speech Macros]. If you sign one macro in the directory, all macros in the same directory will also be "signed" and can be used.

[Advanced] Menu Macros

It is beyond the scope of this tutorial to summarize the operation of the other two macro templates. For interesting examples of macros, including those prepared with the [Advanced] component, (insert MXL to create sophisticated Speech Macros), search for Rob's Rhapsody:

http:// blogs.msdn.com/b/roach/.

Under Popular Tag, select Macros. Review the rest of the site as well. For a computer that talks back visit:

> Talking with pc : Make your computer respond like Jarvis ! | epic ...
> https://epicnewsnetwork.wordpress.com/.../talking-with-pc-make-you-computer-respo... ▼
> Jun 7, 2013 - So go ahead and download Windows Speech Recognition Macros here. Before you install the Macros, make sure your microphone is attached ...

A user's guide, **WSR Macros: The User's Guide** is also available. It contains additional guidance on working with Macros. Check for additional information on it and other subjects on the MSSpeech Forum website.

~CHAPTER ELEVEN~

Switching and Navigating

The focus thus far has been on using Microsoft Speech Recognition to prepare documents. As Quick Guides, we prepared Table 1 Column A and B and Table 2 Column A and B, Page 51 and Page 88.

Table 2 Column B will represent a departure. Here we will discuss some additional navigational functions of speech recognition: within applications on the computer, and on the Internet.

Not all of us react in the same way. If you have used several computers, you know they do not respond in the same way either.

Accordingly, some suggestions that worked for us while preparing this tutorial may not work for you or work well on your computer. If you have difficulty, try alternatives.

Navigation Within the Computer

We will first review navigating between applications and programs on the computer. Windows Speech Recognition makes it easy to switch between active applications/programs.

[Start]

We are already aware that applications and programs can be opened by [Start] or [Open] and the (name) of (the application). Once open, even if the application does not allow speech recognition, often menus can be opened with Speech Recognition. Some submenus can be selected and opened using [Show Numbers [Go] (Up/Down) (# of lines) and finalized by either [OK], [Click], or [Double click].

An alternative is the [Mouse Grid] which can zero in on a link, which can be opened by [Click] or [Double Click].

[Open] (From Desktop)

[Open] will open another application even when composing in a compatible speech recognition editor or word processor. We have found it more efficient to use [Open] or [Start] [Commands] to open an application from the desktop, because there is less likelihood that the [Command] will be confused if spoken while composing. Menus on the desktop also makes it easier to identify an application.

[Open] (Control Panel)

Even those who use a computer primarily for word processing can benefit from opening the [Control Panel]. When used with Windows Speech Recognition it is the key to check microphone settings. This was covered in an earlier chapter. It can be navigated with a combination [Commands], [Show Numbers] or the [Mouse Grid] and the associated navigational [Commands].

[Switch] (Application)

The [Command] (Switch to) is used when two or more applications (programs) are open. This combination enables you to switch back and forth between applications, without pressing and holding the [Alt] key and the [Tab] key to move among open applications.

[Switch] (Application) [Switch to] (Desktop)

In Windows 10 there is a [Task View] icon next to the Cortana circle. It looks like a window with a shutter on each side. If [Left] clicked it will show what applications are open. Select the appropriate one by a [Left] click.

The [Command] [Switch to] (Desktop) is more responsive than [Switch to] an (Application) while in another application. Use [Switch] (to Desktop) first, and then for example [Open] (WordPad).

[Pick a Program]

This opens a window [Pick a program], which shows what is open on your computer. To make it easier to recognize what is open, name and save files that have been opened in the same application.

For example, if you have two files open in [WordPad], if they are not named [Pick a program] will show them with a number in front of them. [Pick a program] will show what Applications/Programs are currently open. It will not summarize content. Give each file a name to identify the content and make it easier to switch back and forth between them.

NAVIGATING THE INTERNET

[Open] (Browsers by name). We have experimented with Microsoft Edge, Internet Explorer, Google Chrome, Mozilla Firefox, and Opera. All of them open after the [Command] (Open) and their name. After opening the browser, set the cursor in the address line. Composea file name in the address line using [Enable dictation scratchpad]. Some browsers are more responsive than others. If that does not work open [Notepad]. Dictate there and [Copy] and [Paste] into the address line. If that does not work with Google Chrome use Search Google.

What you can do with any of them after they open depends on you, your computer, and the browser. Usually you can navigate using [Show Numbers] or [Mouse Grid].

A Tip: When frequently using websites, set bookmarks on the

Bookmarks Bar of your browser. Check your browser to determine if it permits this.

Bookmarks Bar

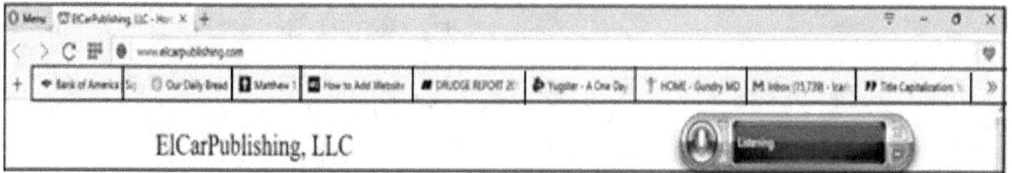

The image above shows a series of bookmarks placed on an Opera browser. Bookmarks designated for the Bookmarks Bar but not able fit in it are stored below the Bookmarks Bar on the [Left] under the Opera (O). These are located elsewhere on other browsers. When the menu is shown navigate by using [Show Numbers].

Bookmarks are on the [Left] side of Google Chrome behind three stacked dots under the X. Review other browsers to determine where they contain this feature. Use [Show Numbers], or the [Mouse Grid] to select entries.

~~END OF SPEECH RECOGNITION TUTORIAL~~

~CHAPTER TWELVE~

Construction and Conversion of Tables

TABLES AND PDF APPLICATIONS

Tables and images are inserted into text to highlight key points in the text. They provide a visual summary of the text, emphasize key information, serve as placeholders and help with recall.

We will present a method of creating tables in a word processor and converting them to PDF images. These are [Copied] and [Pasted] into an image editor. There they are edited, both as to size and quality, and saved in one of eight image formats. These images can then be [Inserted] into documents.

This is an extra step but image files produce more stable tables. Although the process may seem unnecessary at first, it produces better-quality tables and after it is learned, it will prove its worth.

A Five-Step Process

To create a table, we will use four applications, a word processor, a PDF creator, a PDF Viewer and an Image Editor.

THE WORD PROCESSOR

We will create tables using Microsoft Word 2013. The procedure will vary somewhat in later editions. Tables can also be produced with, OpenOffice, and LibreOffice. WordPad does not have this feature.

We chose Word 2013 because we can enter data into the table cells with Windows Speech Recognition. We can dictate text in Word 2002 or later, but not in OpenOffice LibreOffice or in Microsoft Word processors before Word 2002. OpenOffice and LibreOffice create tables in much the same way as Word 201andand3. With some modification, the following steps will work with them as well.

Whether using Word or another word processor, the table shell itself is created manually. If not using a compatible Microsoft Word processor also enter data into the cells manually.

Step One

First prepare a separate document with narrow borders. We use 11 x 8.5 inches. We use a larger page size to create the table with larger fonts, so when it is copied the fonts will be clearly displayed. If creating a table with a preponderance of rows use the portrait view. If emphasis is on columns use landscape.

As an example, we are showing a simple outline of a table with three columns and two rows. As you can see, it occupies all of the space between the [Left] and [Right] margins.

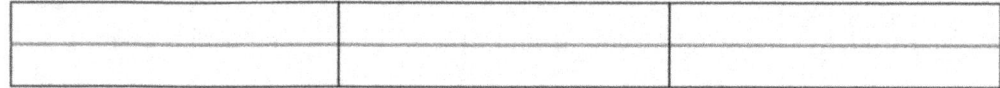

To practice, create a table with at least the above features on a large page size in landscape orientation. Use [Insert] [Table] and then [Insert Table]. If you wish to create a larger table with more rows and columns use the same procedure.

If you are creating a Table to be used in a document feel free to create as many rows and columns as is necessary.

Step Two

After completing the table, enter your text in the cells with speech recognition or by typing. Experiment with the font and the size of font. You can adjust the size of the font to fit the cells. We are providing an example to show what happens if too much data is included in a cell. We initially created too much data in Column 3 in the first table below. We decreased the size of the font in the second table by only 6 sizes, from 26 to 20. Note the change in appearance. If a significant amount of data is needed, the fonts can be reduced until the data occupies the same height as the other columns.

Do not change cell borders until the data has placed in the cells. Adjust both the fonts and the cells. The borders between the columns are adjusted by placing the cursor on a border, grasping it, and moving it either [Right] or [Left] depending on which border needs to be moved. Experiment with this process until the table is balanced.

Creating and Adjusting Size of Cells

Column 1	Column 2	Column 3
Test Table	Garamond 26 Font	Adjust Borders too much content adds another line. Decrease contents or change the size of the font.

Column 1	Column 2	Column 3
Test Table	26 Font	Adjust Borders. Too much content adds another line. Decrease content or change the size of the font (20).

Review the above images. You may have to adjust the fonts and the borders several times before it looks right.

Step Three
Creating a Separate Title

You have the option of creating a title in the table or as a separate image. There are advantages in creating these separately. If done separately, you can control the size and appearance of the title. They will be combined to create one image when copied. If you create them on the same page, leave a couple of lines between the title and the table for editing.

Titles are created as a [Table], or with the [Text Box] using Word.

Creating in the [Text Box] with Word will create a white margin between the cell color and the margin as shown below when the [Paint Bucket] and a color is selected. Creating it in [Text Box] gives it a more distinctive look and makes it stand out from the rest of the completed table. The title below has been edited. If created in [Table] it would not have the white margin.

The location of the [Text Box] will vary depending on the Word edition. In 2013 use [Insert], then [Text Box]. For the Title, select a font that is larger than the one in the table. Experiment with this, because if the text is too large, it will not fit well in the box.

Example of Title Created with [Text Box]

Creating Tables

Experiment with [Table] and [Text Box] in other word processors. To color the background in Word, LibreOffice and OpenOffice use the paint bucket symbol.

When done, move the sides of the box to allow text to fill the box. Choose the background color from the pouring bucket icon usually at the top of the menu. For Word 2013 this is at [Home] (Bucket symbol) (Tables and Borders). It may be elsewhere in other editions.

In any word processor, if you have difficulty adding the background color it can be added when editing the PDF file after it is converted to a PNG or JPEG image. For that matter the Title can be created in Paint.NET, or the image editor of your choice.

An example of a Modified Table which was converted to a PDF file, then [Copied] and [Pasted] into an image editor is shown on the next page. The Title was created in the same document. Additional spacing was created between it and the table. They were transformed to a PDF file which was [Pasted] into Paint.NET. There the components were edited, placed together and enclosed with an outside border. The result was [Pasted] into this book.

Title and Table with Border

Creating Tables		
Column 1	Column 2	Column 3
Row 1	R1 C2	R1 C3

Formatting Cell Borders

As part of the [Table] toolbar in Word 2013, you have the option of 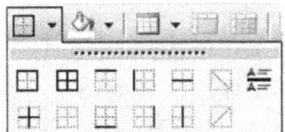 selecting or unselecting the cell borders. In the top table on page 116, we first highlighted and then eliminated all borders in column 1 and 2. We again highlighted the top, bottom, and [Left] and [Right] borders. We eliminated the border between the rows. Start by eliminating all borders in all rows and columns that are being altered and then reintroduce those borders that complete the desired pattern. This will require experimentation.

Open Office has a similar feature. It can be found after you format the table. The border feature is behind the icon to the [Right] of the [AutoFormat] icon. It is labeled [Table Properties]. For LibreOffice use [Table]. It is found at [Table] [Properties [Borders].

Each of these word processors have additional options for the enhancing the appearance of tables. Become familiar with the alternatives present in the of the one(s) you use to add variety to your documents.

The variations are not always evident. Explore the menus to find them. They are not in the same menus in all processors.

Step Four
Creating a PDF File

A PDF (portable document format) is a format developed by Adobe. It reproduces all the elements of a document and saves them as a digitalized file that can be viewed, edited, or printed by any operating system. Others use this technology and many PDF applications with various options have been created.

A PDF document, or part of it, can be [Copied] and [Pasted] into an Image Editor. There it can be edited and saved as an image file.

The advantage of using an image file instead of a "raw" table is that an image is more stable and will not be distorted when the printed. In addition, the DPI (Dots per Inch), can be adjusted to increase the quality of the image.

Consider a PDF application as another printer. After it is downloaded, it will appear when [Print] is chosen to print a document. Instead of printing to the printer, select the PDF file to create a PDF file. The above images were created with Primo PDF by Nitro. Microsoft Word, OpenOffice and LibreOffice have their own PDF file applications under [Export]. Use them instead if you prefer.

Save to the same file, with a similar name as your document. In our example, on page 115 we showed a table with three columns and two rows. The ones that appear in this document were created on a letter size page (8.5 x 11 inches) in landscape mode.

The second table on page 115 shows two font sizes, necessary because of the amount of data placed in the second row of Column 3. Both tables were first converted to PDF files then [Pasted] into Paint.NET for editing.

We converted the PDF files to JPEG image files instead of PNG. The original tables were [Saved], but the image files were placed in the document using [Insert].

PDF APPLICATIONS

We have used several PDF Applications Acrobat by Adobe, Primo PDF by Nitro, Nitro Reader 5, PDFill PDF and Imager Writer (Free) as well as Microsoft Word [Export] PDF/XPS Document.

We have used the FREE Primo PDF by Nitro so often it is an automatic first choice for us for smaller projects. We discovered it first and have used it for several years. We have experimented with the other applications and the user may find any one of these, or one of their choice, works just as well for them.

Primo PDF by Nitro

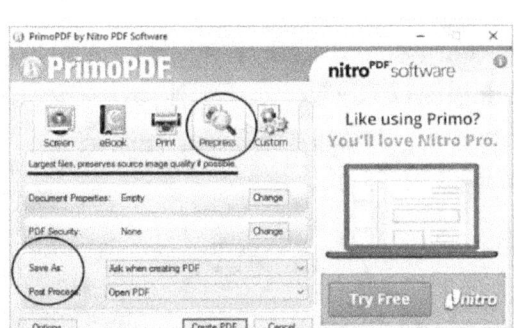

Users of Microsoft Word 2003 and current editions use Microsoft [Print to PDF] or [Export] (Create PDF/XPS, under General √ PDF/A-1a, Standard…) that will emulate the page size set in Microsoft Word. Similar features are found in both OpenOffice and LibreOffice. Use them to convert documents for creating books.

PDF-XChange

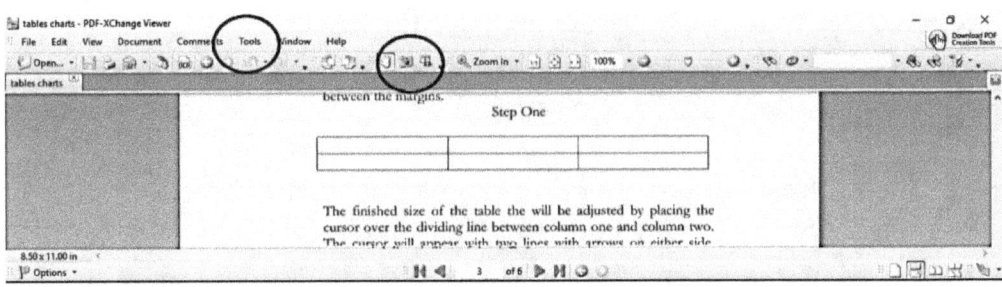

Very early we discovered and continue to use PDF-XChange by Tracker Software as a PDF viewer. Old habits work for us. Like Primo PDF, we have used it so long it is our go-to choice. The features we use most are the [Snapshot Tool] and the [Typewriter]. We would be confident using other applications as well.

PDF Viewers

In the image on page 119 we show a [Print Screen] of PDF-XChange. We have circled the [Tools] and [Camera]. The markup tools appear under [Tools].The [Snapshot Tool], which looks like a camera, is used to select an entire PDF image, or a part of it. Using the cursor to outline the selection, use [Copy] and [Paste] it into an Image Editor.

Use a reliable PDF viewer for keeping track of and editing PDF files. We have also used Nitro Reader 3 by Nitro, the PDFill PDF series and also Adobe Acrobat Reader DC.

Step Five
Creating Images

We have shown how to create tables and how to convert them first to PDF files then to images which can be included in documents. Learn how to download pictures from your digital camera to your computer and create a file folder for them. Use public domain images if they will help tell the story. If you have access to a scanner, you can scan printed images directly into a Picture File.

Whenever you create or edit images, save them with an identifying name and create suitable files to house them. If you consistently lose track of them buy **Ultrafilesearch**, which when we first used it was free. Excellent tool, search for their site for prices.

Snipping Tool

As we have already discussed, Snipping Tool is part of your operating system. For Surface, you can download a Snipping Tool from the

Windows Store. This is a convenient way to capture an image, or a portion of text on the monitor. It can be copied directly into a basic document. If the document is for publication, however, the image, which appears to be only 96 DPI, needs to be changed to 300 DPI.

This will affect the quality of an image. Use it only for smaller images. They can be [Saved] and [Edited] with an Image Editor, where they can be sharpened if a better quality image is not created or found.

CHAPTER FOURTEEN
Using Paint.NET

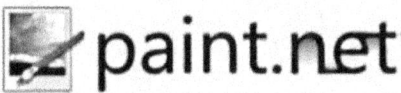

This free program in many respects emulates Adobe Print Shop, Paintshop Pro and other similar commercial photo editing software. Because of this, learning Paint.NET also serves as a primer on how to navigate the principal functions of them as well.

There are several other free image editors we could have used to demonstrate working with images. Paint.NET, however, has long been our primary image editor. For our purposes it will perform all of the functions needed to modify images for inclusion in written documents. Since it is free all readers will be able to download it or a similar free one from Microsoft Store.

Down Load Paint.NET

Use one of the familiar search engines, DuckDuckGo, Google, Bing or another search engine to locate and download Paint.NET, open it and follow as we review some of its features.

IMPORTANT NOTE ON VISTA AND WINDOWS 7

Microsoft ended mainstream support of Vista on April 10, 2012, and extended support April 11, 2017. Mainstream support of Windows 7 ended on January 13, 2015, but extended support will continue until January 14, 2020. It is recommended by many technical people that these operating systems be upgraded for security purposes.

With the exception of the first two Microsoft Surface tablets, which have a unique operating system, most applications we will review work on Vista through Windows 10. Some, however, because of updates, may no longer work on Vista or Windows 7.

OldApps.com

Fortunately, there is a website, OldApps.com, which provides earlier editions of popular applications that work on Vista or Windows 7. For example, we have used Paint.NET on Vista systems, but found the current edition does not work with Vista. We found an earlier edition, Paint.NET v3.5.11, on that site, that does.

Review that site if you are looking for a specific application that is not otherwise available for Vista or Windows 7. We cannot guarantee the legality or quality of these applications. We did, however, download Paint.NET from that site for a Vista operating system and features we will discuss worked on it.

Windows Speech Recognition and Windows Speech Recognition Macros work well with both of these operating systems. They also work with Microsoft Word beginning with 2002. Word is not free, and is not necessary, but is helpful in completing our exercises.

If you have either of these operating systems and they continue to work well, continue to use them at your own discretion, without any warranties or guarantees from us, but protect them with antivirus and frequently optimize your computer.

Summary of Paint.NET Menus

	Paint.NET Menu			
File	Edit	Image	Layers	Effects
(New)	(Copy)	(Resize)	(Add new layer)	(Photo)
(Open)	(Undo)	(300 DPI)		(Sharpen)
(Open Recent)	(Cut)	(6 x9)		(Adjust)
(Save as)	(Paste)	(X = W)		

Use the summary to become familiar with the features we will discuss. When Paint.NET is first opened it shows menu items at the top and also displays a large canvas area. All editing takes place in the can-

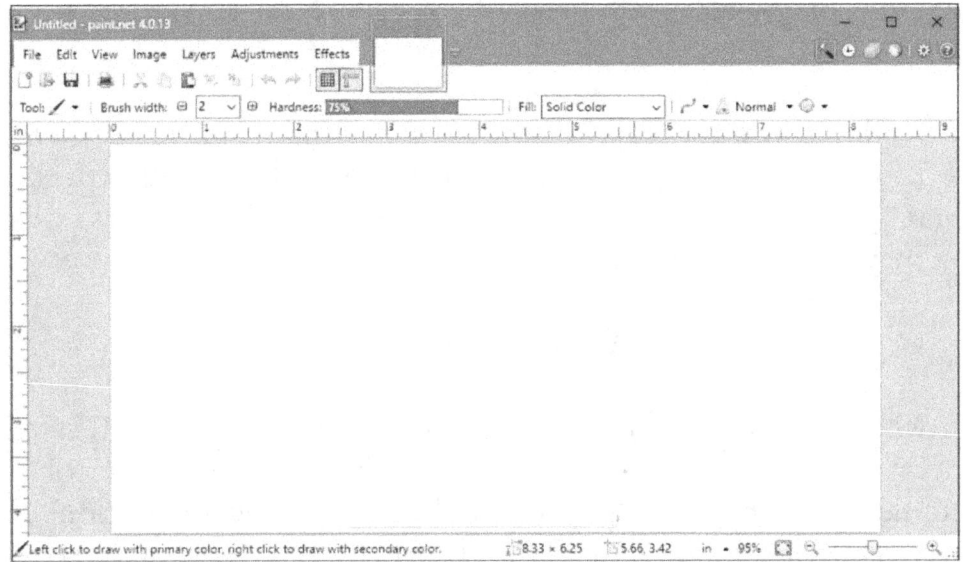

vas area which is blank in the above image. We have also created a composite image below to show the location and appearance

The Canvas Followed by a Composite Image

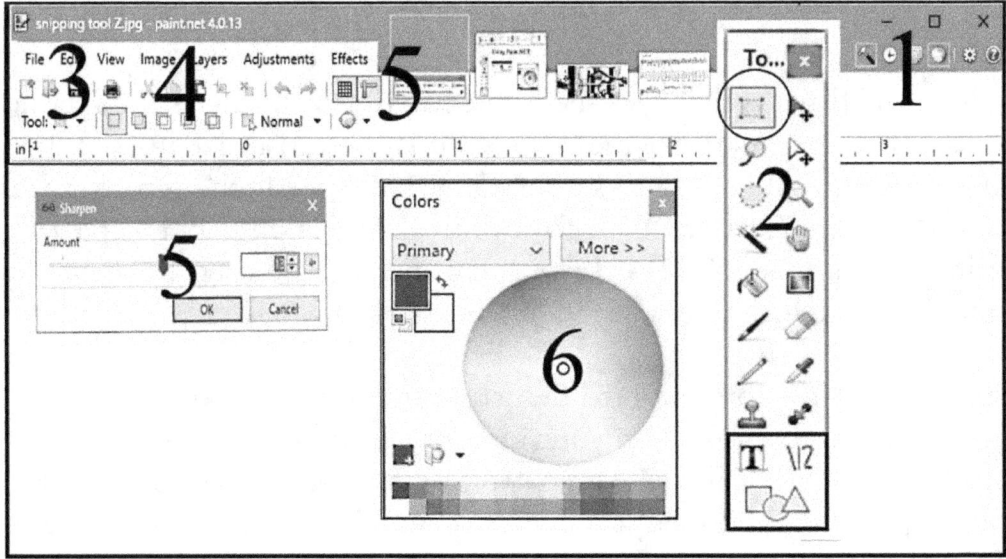

125

of the menu items we will be discussing. We will only discuss those tools that we will use in this exercise. To introduce the tools we will use, we have numbered some menu items and tools and have superimposed them on an image of the Paint.NET application on the last page.

Paint.NET saves images by default as PNG files. When you [Save] a file it will save as a PNG image unless you select another format. There are other features of this image editor we will not discuss which you may wish to explore later.

Rectangle Select Tool

We will mostly use two tools. The principle tool will be the [Rectangle Select] tool (**2**) which is opened by clicking on the image of the hammer (**1**) in the upper [Right] hand corner of the application. The [Rectangle Select] tool is located at the top of the [Left] column of the tool menu. It appears as a square.

We have emphasized it by placing it within a circle. This is used to surround an area to [Copy] or sometimes to [Cut] out portions of it. We will use it mostly to [Resize] and format an image.

Resize

Under the [Image] file (**4**) is the Submenu [Resize]. This is the second most used tool. As the name suggests it is used to resize images. Just as importantly, it is used to set the DPI (Dots per Inch) density of an image. The industry standard for printing images on paper, especially printed books, is 300 DPI. Lower densities can be used for e-Books images where it can be set at 95 DPI.

We will edit a photograph to demonstrate how to modify an image. [Open] a photograph from your picture file. If you do not have one, find and download one. [Copy], [Save] and [Open] it with Paint.NET using [File] then [Open]. It will open with a preset [Width] and Height].

Using [Image] and [Resize] review the properties of the image. When editing an image check √ the [Maintain aspect ratio] box which will ensure that all modifications to the image will maintain the same relative [Width] and [Height]. While we will be working with a photograph, the same the procedure will apply to any image.

Editing a Photograph

First estimate the finished size of the new image. It is better to make it slightly larger than too small. It is easier to reduce it in a document than enlarge it. An entire image or a portion of it can be a resized. In both cases the selected image will first be outlined using the [Rectangle Select Tool] introduced above.

 Using the cursor, place the lower [Right] 90 degree angle of the [Rectangle Select Tool] at the upper [Left] corner of the area that is selected. Consider it as a type of scanner that collects whatever it passes over. Move it diagonally 135° ↘ to the bottom [Right] corner until the selected area has been totally outlined.

The process can also begin in the upper [Right] corner, moving it diagonally 135° ↙ to the lower [Left] corner. In either case the selected area will appear shaded. In the example above, we selected only a portion of the photograph for [Resizing]. We have emphasized the size of the selected area with a dotted black line. In Paint.NET it will have the appearance of white and black dashes. [Copy] changes.

Then use [File] to open [New]. A blank image will appear on the canvas. This will be followed by a window titled [New]. It will show a number of variables. Simply [OK] it. We will set the parameters later.

Use [Edit] and the submenu [Paste] to place the captured image into the [New] file window. The area that was selected and copied will now be housed in the [New] file. After [New] is OK'ed, it will no longer be shaded or outlined. Use [Resize] to set the size and DPI of the image.

Formatting the Image

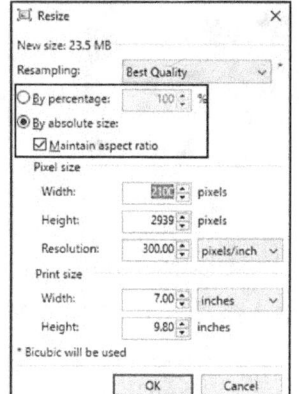

There is one constant that needs to be set for all images that are inserted into a printed document for publication. It is to set the resolution at 300 DPI. It is important when an image is first [Opened] or [Pasted] to √ check this and the [Maintain Aspect Ratio] box.

Calculate the [Width] dimension of your picture or image. When editing an image use [Image] ▶ [Resize] to adjust the size. When an image is [Resized] maintain the aspect ratio that was established when it was first opened or [Pasted]. Because the ratio of [Width] and [Height] has already been established, it is only necessary to change the [Width]. The [Height] will automatically be established.

Inserting Within Text?

If the image will be placed into a line of text, it will be necessary to create white margins on all sides of the image adjacent to the text. Make these margins about the size of the font used in the main text. This will separate the image from the text.

As a general rule, if an image spans across the entire width of the page it often is not necessary to create these margins. If it does not look right consider creating white margins on the top and bottom.

Creating Margins

It is important when an image is first [Opened] or [Pasted] or [Saved] to check √ the [Maintain Aspect Ratio]. Use the [Rectangle Select Tool] to create a narrow margin on all sides. This must be done individually on each side. [Delete] the area that is selected. Make them a uniform width on all sides. You do not need to outline the overall image in black as shown here. But you can if you wish. Be consistent. Before [Saving] use [Image] [Resize] and double-check the parameters. Set the resolution at 300 DPI.

It is not always necessary to employ a title. Whether one is given is at the discretion of the designer. If one is used it is usually centered and capitalized.

What to Capitalize? Capitalize My Title

Questions on capitalization? First, set up your caption. Easily solved on https://capitalizemytitle.com/. [Copy] and [Paste] into Capitalize My Title. Selections are Title Case, AP style APA style, Chicago style, MLA style and more. After the process is completed, [Copy] the result and [Paste] into your document. There are other similar apps.

Working with Microsoft Word, OpenOffice or LibreOffice, images are introduced into the document using [Insert]. The process is generally the same but the menus operate somewhat differently. Become familiar with the one you are using. We usually insert images to the left margin below a full line of text. For variety they can be aligned with the right margin. The settings for the exact placement of an image within the text differs between word processors.

After the images are inserted they may need to be readjusted to allow 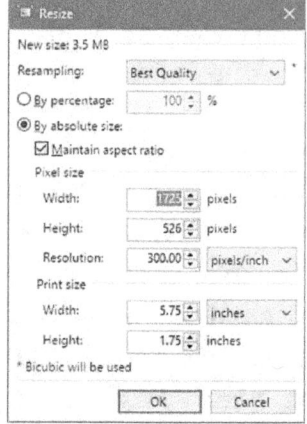 the text to wrap around them. If you need to change the dimensions of your picture or image, again use [Image] ▶ [Resize] to adjust the size. Maintain 300 DPI for images to be printed on paper. A lesser DPI is OK for electronic images.

In Microsoft Word, [Right click] on the image with the cursor to open [Wrap Text], then [Tight] Box or [In Line with Text]. Or click on the icon to the upper right of the image to open [LAYOUT OPTIONS] and make essentially the same selections. Some editions of Word will vary. OpenOffice and LibreOffice have similar options. If using them become familiar with them.

There are three ways to modify placement. (1) Place the cursor in the middle of the image. The [Move image tool] will appear. The [Move image tool] is a rotated X with points on all four ends of the X. Shown here as white with a black border, it is often black with a white border. This may appear instead and is used in the same way. Pressing the [Right] mouse button over the image and holding it will lock the cursor on the image. Drag the image to its final location. When there release the mouse. Sometimes it will require a little nudging.

(2) There is a small box containing an image similar to the [Move image tool] below and to the [Right] of the image. This can be used to move the image. In addition, if you place the cursor below the box a curved section of a circle with arrows on each end and will appear. This is used to rotate the image.

Be careful when inserting an image into another image that you do not inadvertently trigger this. You will end up with an image that is beginning to rotate. If this happens use [Edit] [Undo].

(3) After being [Pasted] the sides of the image will have markers in each corner and in the middle on each side. To make a smaller image these are typically grasped by the cursor, usually at the bottom [Right] and pulled inward 135° ↖ up. To expand the image the corner would be grasped and pulled down ↘135°.

This can create two problems. First, using this tool can distort the image and make it look out of proportion. Second, the 300 DPI will be decreased if the image is made larger. If you need to make it larger, since it presents a change in the DPI, determine the new size. Use [Resize] to enlarge the image to the correct size and maintain 300 DPI.

When properly sized [Save] the file with an appropriate name. The same name can be used, but add an appropriate symbol B, C, D, etc. to designate it has been altered. [Reinsert] in the document.

Inserting Images into WordPad

Pictures or images can be placed in the text of WordPad. While [Word wrap] can be can used for text, there is no provision for wrapping text around images. Include them when creating a document to show their presence. When editing the document with another processing application it may be necessary to [Reinsert] the images from the [Saved] image file.

Placing an Image into Another Image

A portion of an image can be [Copied] and [Pasted] back into the donor image. This is done to emphasize a portion of an image, such as a face, by enlarging it and placing it back into the original picture.

First [Save] the original image. Do not make any changes directly to the original image. [Save] it again with a new name as a working file. We use the same file name plus B, C, D, etc.

Use the same procedure we discussed earlier to select an area which will then be [Copied] as a new file. Use [Copy] then [New] to create the new file. [Save] with same name including B, C, or D, etc. to differentiate, yet associate it with the original image.

[Copy] then [Paste] the new image into the donor image. After [Pasting] it has to be positioned. Use the [Move image tool] to place. If too large, use [Undo] to back out and [Save] with smaller dimensions. If too small use [Undo]. Increase the size and [Save]. Maintain the 300 DPI. Reintroduce into the donor image again. Use [Move image tool] to place, [Save] with a unique name.

To Improve Clarity

To sharpen an image, use [Effect] (Photo) (Sharpen) after [Resize] and before [Save]. This helps sharpen an image. When using observe the white area within loops in a word. If they start to blur, the slider, which controls the degree of sharpening, is set too high (scale of 0 to 20). Adjust until the loops are clearer. We usually set the slider at 7 or 8 for 300 DPI images. In some cases if no distortion it is set higher.

Sharpen

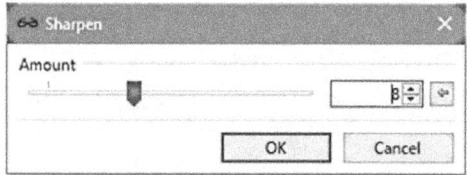

Open Recent

Paint.NET has an [Open Recent] feature under the [File] tab. This enables reopening images that have been [Saved] during a session. They will appear in chronological order. Also, when you initially save images the date they were last modified will appear in the file directory. For ease in finding, always give images a unique name and it is helpful if you also include the date they were prepared.

Text and Shapes

[Open Recent] is an important feature of Paint.NET when adding text or Shapes to an image. We always work from [Open Recent]. If in doubt [Save] the image and reopen it from [File] [Open Recent]. We have had more success when adding text done this way. When setting up text Paint.NET opens with the default Calibri 12. We generally use Times New Roman or Garamond. It is not unusual to have to begin with a 36 Font or higher.

When using Shapes the default [Brush Width] is 2. If it is difficult to see the Shape increase this so you can clearly see them. Decrease when finally placed. They do not look good if they are too wide. Narrow lines however are difficult to see when placing.

Obtaining Images

There are numerous places to obtain good images. Digital photographs can be taken with cameras, smartphones, laptops and many desktop computers. These can be [Uploaded] and [Saved] in files on your computer. Stock images and photographs can be obtained on the Internet.

Unfortunately many stock images or photographs are indexed as "free" but in fact are not. To the occasional noncommercial user this appears a "bait and switch" tactic. (In some cases it might be.)

The problem is these sites are used by commercial customers who understand they either buy a license or pay royalties to use these images. To them it is not "bait and switch," it is the way they do business. The alternative is to produce their own images or photographs.

If you search, you can occasionally find an original, public domain image, which is free to use. In addition, some owners of images and photographs voluntarily modify their rights and place them in what is called Creative Commons, or CC0. (CC + Zero.)

Rights to those materials are relinquished either totally or with some restrictions, and can be used without paying a fee or royalties as long as the restrictions are followed. Some of these can be used commercially, but be careful to read closely for any restrictions.

Look for Public Domain and CC0 Images

To understand some of the issues involved in using Public Domain and Creative Commons (CC0) images and pictures, and to avoid problems, began with https://en.wikipedia.org/wiki/Wikipedia:Public domain image resources. Read this to find out how you can to use Public Domain and CC0 images and photographs. This will save unnecessary confusion and the possibility of inadvertently infringing on someone's copyright.

Also this site lists more than four dozen Public Domain and CC0 sources, arranged by size of collection, largest first. Some are totally free without restrictions, but some do have restrictions which must be honored.

Some CC0 contributors do not permit using images or photographs for front or back covers. If you are seeking images or photographs for covers be aware of this potential restriction and do not use them.

Some vendors also show their images and pictures there. They usually are not "free." Don't confuse them with the public domain and CC0 images and pictures. This is also true of the images or photographs found elsewhere.

There are six sites where totally free images can be downloaded, www.postermywall.com and www.pexels.com. Commercial images appear in the following. They are www.ushistoryimages.com, / www.open-clickart.com./ /www.clker.com, and www.publicdomainq.net (If necessary translate the Japanese narrative.)

Images and photographs in the Public Domain can be embellished to look better. Improving one, however, does not grant ownership rights, and the improved image still remains in the public domain.

Summary

First, [Open] the image. Then use [Rectangle Select] on the [Tool] menu, to mark the area to edit, by dragging the mouse over the area. Under [Edit] use [Copy]. Follow with [New], then [Paste]. [Resize] and [Save] with a descriptive name. [File] [Open Recent] or further editing.

~CHAPTER FIFTEEN~
Recapturing Written Documents

OCR (Optical Character Recognition)

Our focus has been on creating original text using Microsoft Windows Speech Recognition. While it excels at creating text it is not designed to recreate text that already exists on a printed page or elsewhere. Optical character recognition applications however do exactly that.

If you have created, but lost an electronic file, but have [Saved] a printed copy of it, OCR enables you to convert the text on that document to digital text so it can be reconstituted in new document.

To better understand the concept, one of the most precise definitions of optical character recognition is given by Wikipedia. It is as follows:

> Optical character recognition (also optical character reader, OCR) is the mechanical or electronic conversion of images of typed, handwritten or printed text into a machine-encoded text, whether from a scanned document, a photo of a document, a scene-photo (for example the text on signs and billboards in a landscape photo) or from subtitle text superimposed on an image (for example from a television broadcast).

This tutorial indirectly had its origin in Optical Character Recognition. Several years ago we used a commercial version of OCR to refurbish an over-copied Xeroxed copy of a typewritten handbook to restore it to a legible Microsoft Word document. This was first converted into a standard 8 ½ by 11 inch document, but was later formatted and printed as a Print-on-demand (POD) book.

Using this method it was not necessary to "retype," or use speech recognition to reproduce most of the document. This not only saved work but with some minor editing also preserved the original structure of the underlying document.

During this project we also discovered Microsoft Windows Speech Recognition. Learning how to use it became the motivation for this tutorial.

FreeOCR – Be Careful!

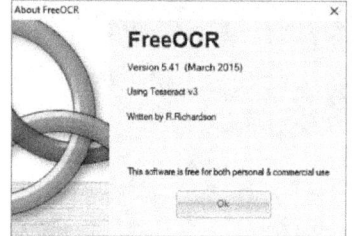

If you search for a free OCR application, you will receive several choices. For a number of years we used a free application which did a good job. We were unable to find it for several months. When we did, we checked it with **Virustotal**. It was suspicious for a virus or adware. We took it off our computers and replaced it with FreeOCR written by RRichards, version 5.41. We have had no problems with the Richards application. The [Help] menu will take you to http://www.paperfile.net/ which will confirm that you have the correct site. But be safe and check it out first.

It is built on the standard Tesseract free OCR engine developed at the Hewlett Packard Laboratories. While we will present a brief summary on how this operates, we encourage those who try OCR for the first time to go to the FreeOCR website for additional instructions which will greatly increase its utility.

OCR is generally used in conjunction with a scanner to convert data on a printed document back to text so it can be incorporated into another document. While that is usually true, it can also be used to convert text directly from images and PDF files.

Example of Mixed Quality

Do not expect excellent results if the document being scanned is of

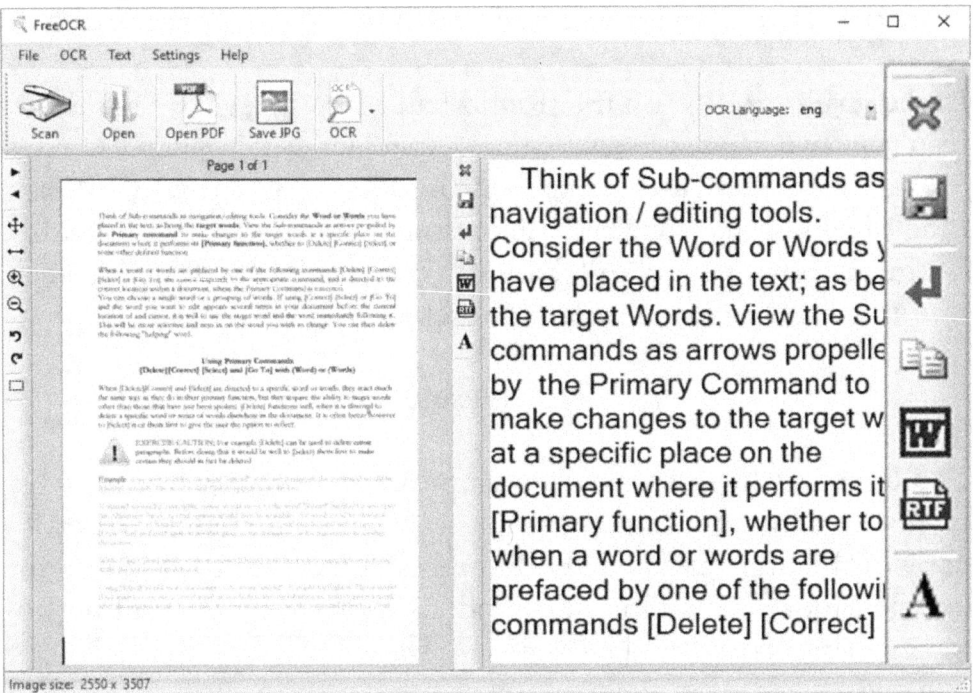

poor quality. While you can obtain results it will require some enhancement to reproduce the original document. See the example above. Check documents for clarity before attempting OCR.

Note the document that was scanned is on the [Left] of the split image above. It is of good quality at the top but of poor quality after the Warning Image, which is part of the original document. For best results the application needs to work with text that is at least the density of a computer printout with black fonts, or dark fonts.

Lighter colors, like light blue, yellow and pink, are less likely to be accurately reproduced as text. It would work better if first converted to JPG images. Enhancing them with an image editor would increase their density. If you have a poor image sometimes it is worth trying to convert the document because you may salvage enough to save reproducing some text and perhaps retain the original form of the document. Experiment.

See the sidebar on the extreme [Right]. This is an enlargement of the center panel of this application. We copied and enlarged it to show more detail. Compare it with the one in the center of the image.

In the result window on the [Right] half of the image, we adjusted the results in two ways. We clicked the capital letter A to increase the size of the fonts. We also clicked on the [Crooked arrow] to [Remove Line Breaks]. Finally we had the option to [Save] by [Export] either to Word, [Export as RTF] or [Copy all Text to Clipboard], or [Paste] into a word processor or editor and [Save].

Application

The use of OCR to convert a document back to digital text saves re-typing or using speech recognition to reproduce the text. Even if the copy of the original dictated or typed document or PDF file is not of excellent quality it still might good enough with some editing to be better than recreating the original. Give OCR a test run.

With the Internet one can quickly gather a considerable amount of information. This can be printed as a PDF file by clicking on the three stacked dots under the (X) in the upper a [right] hand corner of the monitor on Google Chrome and elsewhere on other browsers. Or using [Ctrl] [Print Screen], it can be copied as an image file and [Pasted] into an image editor. Either it can be [Saved] for processing later, or using OCR can be converted to digital text for review and editing.

Avoid the temptation to claim ownership or improperly use copyrighted material. Most authors or publishers will permit a small representation of their work to be quoted. If you have any questions obtain permission from the author or publisher. Don't press the envelope too far on this.

Handwriting OCR

As part of this study, we also downloaded a 14 day trial version of a Handwriting OCR program. This represented several steps backwards for us because it required writing by hand in block letters or cursive handwriting some 300 to 500 words.

For obvious reasons the application did not discriminate between letters that touched. Cursive characters were out. Our handwriting, even when printing, is worse than our typing. Considering the time it took to hand print these pages it is easier and quicker to simply use Windows Speech Recognition to transcribe written notes.

~CHAPTER SIXTEEN~
Special-Purpose Applications

SCRIVENER - YWRITER6

Scrivener

We discovered Scrivener and yWriter4, 5 and now yWriter6, while doing research for a novelist. To become more familiar with programs of special interest to novelists, we researched and also downloaded a 30-day free trial version of Scrivener and a free version of yWriter4. From their website, Scrivener's describes their product as follows:

Writing a novel, research paper, script or any long-form text involves more than hammering away at the keys until you're done. Collecting research, ordering fragmented ideas, shuffling index cards in search of that elusive structure – most writing software is fired up only after much of the hard work is over.

Enter Scrivener: a word processor and project management tool that stays with you from that first, unformed idea all the way through to the final draft. Outline and structure your ideas, take notes, view research alongside your writing and compose the constituent pieces of your text in isolation or in context. Scrivener won't tell you how to write—it just makes all the tools you have scattered around your desk available in one application.

We would describe this as an incredible project management tool. It is not free but sells for a modest $40.00 – $45.00. It is a complex application. Without in any way debasing the value and utility of Scrivener, it is not easy to learn. Many reading this may already be familiar with and already use it. Others who are not need to know about it and experiment with it.

While Scrivener is a very popular application and is successfully used by many writers. Some would-be, and many present authors may not be familiar with it. We suggest they visit their website, download the 30-day free trial, and give it a fair trial.

yWriter6

yWriter4, now yWriter6, like Scrivener, addresses the same issues of interest to novelists and writers of complicated manuscripts. It is a free application but that is not the only reason for looking at it.

It is not a carbon copy, of Scrivener, but it is far easier to learn. It does not require as much study, experimentation and experience to master. For many, especially new novelists, it will accomplish the same task and yWriter6 is FREE. Visit the website www.spacejock.co for detailed information. Its author, Simon Haynes, summarizes it as follows:

> yWriter is a word processor which breaks your novel into chapters and scenes, helping you keep track of your work while leaving your mind free to create. It will *not* write your novel for you, suggest plot ideas or perform creative tasks of any kind. yWriter was designed by an author, not a salesman!
>
> If you're just embarking on your first novel a program like yWriter may seem like overkill. I mean, all you have to do is type everything into a word processor! Sure, but wait until you hit 20,000 words, with missing scenes and chapters, notes all over your desk, characters and locations and plot points you've just added and which need to be referenced earlier ... it becomes a real struggle. Now imagine that same novel at 40,000 or 80,000 words! No wonder most first-time writers give up.
>
> I realise Word, OpenOffice and other modern word processors have outlining features, but they don't have snapshot backups to sequential files like yWriter does. Roll back scenes to where they were half an hour ago, or re-read a version from four months ago - yWriter stores them all, automatically.
>
> yWriter6 is free to download and use, but you're encouraged to register your copy if you find it useful.

yWriter4

Part of the motivation for this tutorial was finding, experimenting and when helpful providing a summary, mostly of FREE applications, that many people producing text are not familiar with.

When we discovered new applications we were also curious if they worked with Windows Speech Recognition. Scrivener did not.

See the image below, which shows text produced by Windows Speech 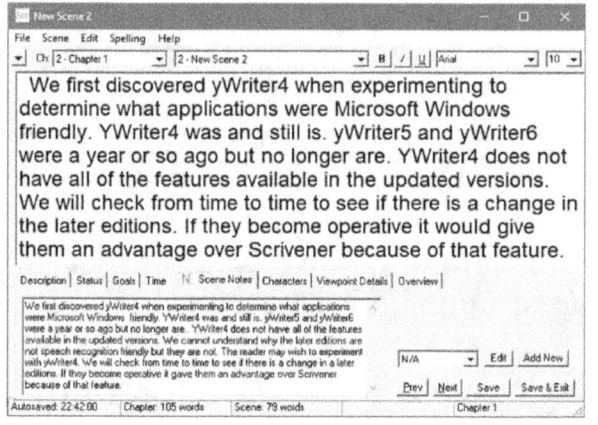 Recognition using yWriter4. It was composed in the lower section, Scene Notes, and [Pasted] above. Speech recognition would not place the text directly into the scene window. While the text had to be [Copied] and [Pasted] into the scene portion it eliminated using another compatible Windows Speech Recognition processor thereby keeping all the text within the application.

YWriter4, 5 and 6 in the past all worked with Windows Speech Recognition. yWriter4 still does with a limitations. For reasons unknown, 5 and 6 no longer do. yWriter4 can still be downloaded from the Spacejock site. Users of Windows Speech Recognition will have a decided advantage over Scrivener both as to functionality as well as cost.

Visit the Website

We recommend that the reader visit www.spacejock.co. There is additional detailed information on the author's webpage; also the yWriter Facebook, twitter, and Wiki accounts; as well as the yWriter discussion group. He also has articles on writing and recommended books on writing.

SUMMARY

We will not be discussing all the features of either of these applications. Using [Cut] and [Paste], documents can be produced with a Windows Speech Recognition compatible word processing application and easily transferred to either of these applications. This increases the usefulness of each since it introduces an element of spontaneity and eliminates a considerable amount of re-typing.

We have experimented with both of these applications. We favor yWriter6. It is free, but that is not the compelling reason. Even though yWriter6 no longer works with Windows Speech Recognition we found that it still is far easier to navigate. We would, however, encourage, the reader to check both of them out and reach their own conclusion. Both can be used for projects other than writing novels.

TEXT-T0-SPEECH

Our principle interest has been Windows Speech Recognition because it enables poor typists, like us, to minimize errors and reduce frustration when producing documents. Speech recognition has a cousin, which is also helpful to writers. This process is known as Text-to-speech, TTS, or speech synthesis.

Text-to-speech is the reverse of Speech-to-Text. Rather than creating text by speaking it, it"reads back" text that has already been produced. Wikipedia again provides us with a working definition.

> Speech synthesis is the artificial production of human speech. A computer system used for this purpose is called a speech computer or speech synthesizer, and can be implemented in software or hardware products. A Text-to-speech (TTS) system converts normal language text into speech.

A bit of history. Legends of machines that imitate human speech go back as far as 1003 AD. The production of five vowel sounds by mechanical means was accomplished by using reeds (such as in contemporary pipe organs) in 1779, followed by a machine in 1791 that could produce consonants as well as vowels. These are interesting facts, but they did not have any practical use.

Enter the Modern Era

Mechanical means gave way to electrical signal processing in the 1930s, when the Bell Labs developed the Vocoder, which automatically analyzed speech. The advances in technology that have created speech recognition have also given rise to Text-to-speech recognition.

Speech Synthesis Voices - SAPI5

Microsoft Corporation and many other companies have developed free text-to-speech applications using speech synthesis. The most recognizable Microsoft creation is the Narrator. The most common Microsoft "voices" are David and Zira.

These "voices" are identified as SAPI voices, which is short for Speech Application Programming Interface. They work with all four Microsoft operating systems we have included in this tutorial. They do a satisfactory job of converting text to speech with other operating systems as well.

Many companies have enhanced the quality of SAPI voices, which produce simulated human speech more accurately than David and Zira. If purchased, they operate with the Text-to-speech applications that work with Microsoft operating systems.

TEXT-TO-SPEECH APPLICATIONS

Our initial interest in Text-to-speech applications was to explore their suitability in conjunction with proofreading documents prepared with Windows Speech Recognition. As part of our research, we initially found more than five Text-to-speech applications that also permitted the creation of text with Windows Speech Recognition.

Since then three of those have been modified and no longer permit this. A remaining free one, Text-to-speech TTS, available from the Microsoft Store still permits creating text with Widows Speech Recognition and it will play it back.

Text to Speech TTS

This does a credible job. NOTE: After creating text [Copy] and

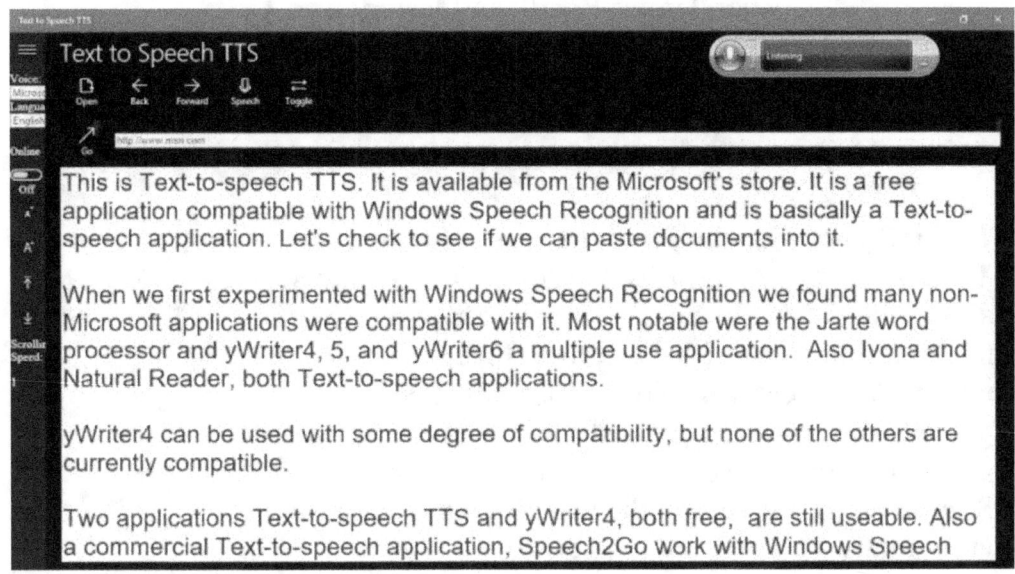

[Paste] into Word or WordPad. During experiments we noted that occasionally it would [Delete] without warning. But it does work and is helpful to proof "read" a document.

TypeIt ReadIt

TypeIt ReadIt is a free Text-to-speech application that used to, but no longer, works with Microsoft Windows Speech Recognition.

Visual Impairment or Reading Disability

TTS is particularly beneficial for people with visual impairments. It also aids people who have difficulty reading. When reconverted into audio files, such as MP3 or .WAV, written documents converted to TTS, can be played back on many sound reproduction devices.

This application was designed by SchoolFreeware.com as an educational typing program for the visually impaired and individuals who either cannot read or desire to improve their reading comprehension. It can be downloaded from this site shown above. It is capable of using the exceptional SAPI5 voices developed by Microsoft and others.

What TypeIt ReadIt Is Designed to Do

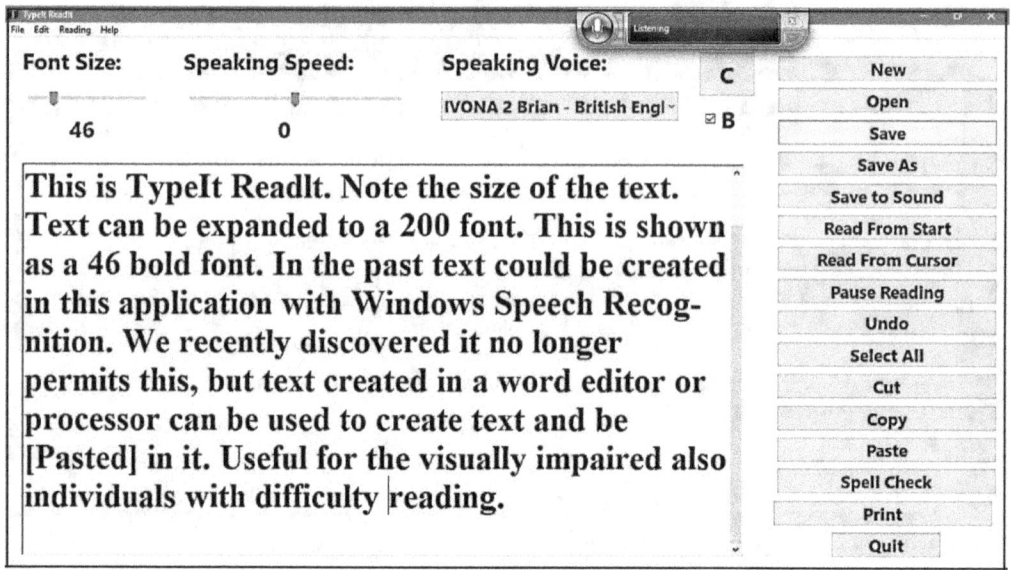

The developers of a program can best describe their program. SchoolFreeware.com on their website describes it as follows:

> TypeIt ReadIt can help users who are visually impaired, cannot read, desire to improve their reading comprehension, or just want to listen to their documents read aloud. TypeIt ReadIt can convert text to a spoken sound file by using its text-to-speech technology. These sound files can be inserted into ITunes, CD, an iPod, PowerPoint, iMovie, Audacity or any other software or device that supports sound files. This can allow students, with speech difficulties, to place the sound files in their presentations, so, they can participate with lessons and class activities.
>
> With TypeIt ReadIt, students can listen to their documents on their iPod. Business professionals can convert their emails, documents, and memos so they can listen to their documents on their car radio while they are stuck in rush-hour traffic. In

addition, TypeIt ReadIt is a useful alternative for young children's typing lessons instead of using a confusing word processor.

TypeIt ReadIt - Making a Good Product Even Better

While this application used to permit the creation of text with Windows Speech Recognition, it no longer does. Documents can be created in compatible processors and [Pasted] into it. This greatly expands its usefulness.

After learning Windows Speech Recognition, it would permit a user, whether a teacher, an assistant, or even individuals who are visually impaired or have difficulty reading, to create individualized programs by composing information with Speech Recognition and [Pasting] the results into this application. The fonts can be enlarged.

This improves their ability to see and aids developing their reading ability. With coaching they could also be taught to create their own documents by typing or using Speech Recognition. This would increase its value as it would enable voice editing during the creation of new documents.

Font Size/Speaking Speed

Note that the font size can be scaled from 10 to 200 and the speaking speed can also be adjusted. This application has many helpful features to assist special people.

TypeIt ReadIt is a significant discovery. The application also converts printed text to .wav sound clips. This is an element that is extremely beneficial not only for its intended audience, but for anyone who would rather listen to than read or review written documents produced by themselves or others.

Download the application and the PDF help file giving more details on how to use it. Playback using the Microsoft SAPI5 voices already part of the Microsoft operating system.

COMMERCIAL PRODUCTS

The initial concept of this tutorial was to include only free applications. That is still our main focus, however, there are some applications and programs we have discovered that a reader might consider adding to their toolkit in the future.

A few years ago, Amazon marketed an excellent Text-to-speech application, Ivona Reader, which also worked very well with Microsoft Windows Speech Recognition. While Amazon does not currently sell or support Ivona Reader, they continue to produce excellent Ivona SAPI5 voices. Ivona has shifted its business from emphasis on Text-to-speech applications to their propriety Bright-Voice technology. It focuses on delivering high-quality Text-to-speech voices.

The Ivona site, however, provides links to Harpo Software, proprietary developer of the Text-to-speech S2G (Speech2Go) application which somewhat replaces Ivona Reader, but is set up in a slightly different format. It also mentions TextAloud3, a Text-to-Speech application by NextUp Technology, LLC. Both produce and provide SAPI5 voices with a variety of different voice characteristics.

S2G – Is Windows Speech Recognition Friendly

S2G (Speech2Go) is one of the commercial versions we discovered which is still compatible with Windows Speech Recognition. It also creates MP3 files of what is produced. Prices on the web site are given in pounds so convert to U.S. dollars. A bit expensive, but interesting.

NaturalReader

This is another application that we have purchased and used for a number of years and at one time was also Windows Speech Recognition compatible. We tested it recently and with the purchased version it is still possible to produce text using Windows Speech Recognition. It can be used for straight dictation, but does not enable correction of the text by voice. This is not a major selling point.

NaturalReader does however have a free web site that enables the user to upload their documents and have it read back by one of several NaturalReader SAPI voices

While not Windows Speech Recognition friendly, it has many has more features that are available both online and in the purchased product. The website is certainly worth visiting and the commercial version has many additional features to make it an item many will consider for purchase.

~CHAPTER SEVENTEEN~

The Information Age

The proliferation of inexpensive computers; the invention of multi-purpose cell phones, smartphones, and similar electronic devices, coupled with FREE word editors and processors, plus easy access to the Internet, has revolutionized the transmission of information.

A virtual army of lay and professional people alike now have affordable, reliable, and ever-expanding choices on when, where and how to connect to this information highway.

We can now receive text, photographs, complicated audio/visual productions, including lifelike pixilated graphics, over the Internet. The computer age has revolutionized what we see, send, read, view, hear, and how we communicate.

Still Communicate with Printed Text?

Notwithstanding all the innovations in visual and audio media, the written text still is a very important part of communication.

The same technology that has opened up access to the Internet has also spawned numerous applications and programs to make it easier to use the PC for creating or retrieving information. Many of these applications and programs, as we have seen, are of high quality and yet they are FREE.

The emphasis of this tutorial has been on Microsoft Windows Speech Recognition and applications that permit creating text with this application. As a free application, it has no rival for creating text on the fly. Technology has however also produced numerous other innovative applications including the following:

MULTIPURPOSE APPLICATION
Calibre

Calibre will open with a Calibre demo. Review it to understand its many features. It has far more ingenious components than we will cover. This application was designed by Kovid Goval. Calibre is best described by its developers:

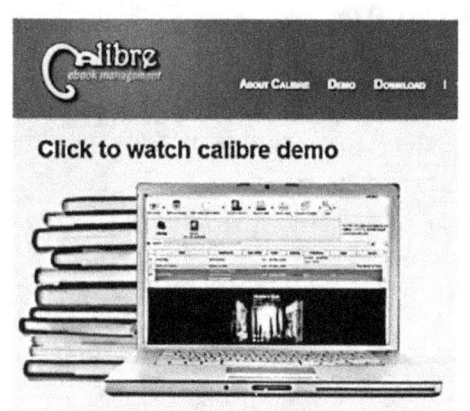

"Calibre is an e-Book library manager. It can view, convert and catalog e-Books in most of the major e-Book formats. It can also talk to many e-Book reader devices. It can go out to the Internet and fetch metadata for your books.

It can download newspapers and convert them into e-Books for convenient reading. It is a cross-platform, running on Linux, Windows and OSX."

This application enables the conversion of text into as many as 18 formats including e-Books, Amazon's Kindle, Barnes & Noble's Nook, and other formats.

If you want to see how your manuscript would look in book form, search for Calibre and read its documentation. We are not suggesting that by converting your documents in Calibre they will meet the standards for commercial printing of e-Books, trade paperbacks, or hardbound books, but they will show you how your manuscript will look in book form. If writing for publication check with your commercial printer for their specifications.

[E-Book Library Manager]

This application is an [E-Book Library Manager]. We have used only a small portion of it. Many readers will find additional features beyond the scope of this tutorial. The website displays a demo. The inquisitive can learn much by visiting the website and downloading the application. Their video explains the details of what they make available.

PAPERBACK AND E-BOOK PUBLISHING OPTIONS

For The Self-Motivated Author

Many seeking easier ways to create documents also have an interest in publishing their work. The same technology that produced the Internet has also made it easier to use the PC for publishing e-Books and Print-on-demand books (POD).

Because it was not economical to print single copies of documents or books using the letterpress or offset printing until digital printing, (POD) was not commercially feasible or available until then.

With new technology and the establishment of POD printing companies documents that have been written, submitted and formatted as a book are electronically stored on the printing company computers. Books are not assembled until they are ordered and paid for. Accordingly, they have no warehousing and no gathering up of books that did not sell.

We have completed a book, *How to Self-Publish for Under $10, I Ought to Write a Book*. Publication has been delayed because of the restructuring of one of the printing companies, but has now been completed and will soon be available from Amazon and Lulu Publishing.

We wrote in because we are familiar with POD and self-publishing. We realized that almost anyone who wants to publish a paperback can, with relatively few instructions and examples, assemble an attractive book themselves. With a little guidance, they can save the expense of hiring a self-publishing service to do what they may not realize they are fully capable of doing.

In some cases, they might need some assistance from someone who has a better working knowledge of Windows Speech Recognition, or more expertise with the keyboard or the Internet. But by self-publishing, even if some help from family or friends is needed, hundreds of dollars can be saved without compromising the quality of the finished work. Anyone helping someone lacking these skills will also profit from learning how relatively easy it is to self-publish.

How to Self-Publish is not about improving writing skills, editing, or proofreading. It is about how to assemble written material so it can be published as an attractive book without entering into a contract, or incurring additional expense. Thus a writer (Self-publisher) can obtain good results without paying for anything, beyond the cost of that book, and copies of books they buy after self-publishing.

It is not intended to be the authority on self-publishing. It is a practical how-to-do guide that everyone who wants to publish a paperback can follow to organize his or her materials to create and self-publish their own book.

Search the Internet under publishing, self-publishing or similar words, and you will find a variety of options. Some will provide details on the cost of printing a single quality paperback of a popular size, with a specific number of pages. Others will ask you to complete a form and apply for their free "How to Publish" book. Or another will request a a down payment of $35.00.

One online printer offers to print a 6x9 32-page paperback book for $5.43, but you must commit to buying 25 copies. As of this writing, $135.78. Want to save money?

How about $4.29 a book? Here you commit to buy 35 copies and pay $150.15. The problem with either is that you must make a commitment and pay for 25-35 copies. Why not a price for one copy? Or none?

Be careful. The inexperienced and uninformed will very likely end up spending far too much to publish. Reputable printers such as CreateSpace, now Kindle Direct Publishing and Lulu, to name just two, will provide instructions and templates to enable a writer to self-publish for well under $10.00 including the cost of the book, shipping and handling, and taxes.

Microsoft Word and several other word processors produce documents suitable for publication. They are usually converted to PDF files and uploaded over the Internet for printing and binding.

Free Tools

As we have shown, if you use a Microsoft operating system from Vista to Windows 10 you already have two free tools from Microsoft to assist in writing a book: Speech Recognition and WordPad.

If you do not have Microsoft Word 2002 or a more current copy of Microsoft Word or Microsoft Office, use WordPad for producing text. WordPad works well for producing text. Photos can be included, but it lacks image formatting tools.

But you can finish your book by [Copying] and [Pasting] your manuscript into OpenOffice, or LibreOffice, a third and fourth FREE tool. They are word processing applications, which have word wrap for images and produce "Mirror Margins" and PDF files.

These are necessary to format a manuscript for a book because facing pages on the [Left] page need to have the same inside margins and outside margins of the same width as those on the [Right] page. An open book has wider margins at the spine (center). WordPad does not create these margins but OpenOffice and LibreOffice do.

If you do any volume of writing and self-publishing, consider buying a genuine copy of at least Microsoft Word 2002. (Word 2003 is even better). Check with eBay. Often legitimate copies sell for well under $30.00. It is not absolutely necessary to use Microsoft Word but for composing with Windows Speech Recognition it is the best choice. It is even better with Word 2013 or later, but will cost more. With Speech Recognition and a compatible copy of Microsoft Word you simply make the job a lot easier and a lot less time-consuming.

Kindle Direct Publishing (KDP), Lulu and Smashwords

Kindle Direct Publishing (KDP), and Lulu are POD publishers they and Smashwords also print e-Books and distribute them on multiple platforms for a portion of the sales. The formatting for an e-Book differs from a print book. A must-read for e-Book self-publishers is *Smashwords Style Guide* by Mark Coker, and the instructions provided by Amazon – Kindle Direct Publishing as well as Lulu.com.

These are self-publishing portals that convert documents prepared on Microsoft Word, WordPad, and Open Office among other word processors into e-Books. You need to follow their guidelines, some formatting is necessary, but both provide instructions.

There are others you find on the Internet, but these three are the best known and provide documented results.

CREATE YOUR OWN WEBSITE

Three decades ago creating and operating a website was a formidable task. It required a working knowledge of HTML, the standard markup language for web pages, and for a professional look, Cascading Style Sheets (CSS), and JavaScript.

Having learned these, the creator of a website still needed to buy a domain name, something like http://www. website.com/name, and gain access to the Internet through a web hosting service called a host. A host is a bank of computers connecting subscribers to the Internet.

The task was made easier with applications that created web pages automatically by producing text and formatting the other elements formerly done by coding. This made websites more practical for a new crop of webmasters. It still required learning a new program, however, acquiring a domain name and a host but it was far easier. These applications not only converted text to HTML, but also made it easier to include pictures, visual and audio content.

That Has Changed

Now it is possible for anyone with some creativity and especially with Windows Speech Recognition skills, to create the text and include pictures and visuals for their websites them self.

We searched for "free web hosting sites." We located and reviewed several that provide the tools to construct a website, and also provide free domain names, and hosting. Explore the Internet for these. After experimenting with several of them, many of which were acceptable, we are using Weebly.com as an example.

Weebly.com - Create Your Own Website

They initially satisfied the conditions we established. 1.) The procedure had to be user-friendly. 2.) It had to have friendly and knowledgeable help-desk personnel. For contact details see below*.

3.) Attractive websites could be created with a relatively short learning curve, and 4.) They had to include FREE domain names and web hosting.

Weebly.com

We chose Weebly because they met these requirements. They are relatively easy to work with. They provide adequate instructions, templates and online help to create a site that has a professional appearance. Following their instructions, a site can be up and running within a few hours.

Once set up, "publishing" updates is a matter of clicking on [Publish]. It is easy to make changes and many additional applications are available. While they provide much for free, Weebly also provides specialized services that can be bought to further enhance your site.

Open with Google Chrome or Mozilla Firefox. For us, it did not work well with Opera or Internet Explorer. Check them out at Weebly http://www.weebly.com.. Enter your e-mail address and password. Go to [Help] and click on Getting Started.

Our Website

We were impressed with Weebly and have transferred our domain to them. We also bought additional services. If you use them or another similar resource, let us know your experience at www.elcarpublishing.com which is currently being updated. When operational, contact us to receive copies of our Quick Guides and other suggestions.

WEEBLY HELP *

While Weebly provides a considerable amount of printed help to assist in designing a website, they do not provide clear instructions on how to contact a technician for unanswered questions.

Technical Support

Following is a summary of the contact procedure we obtained from a Weebly technician. First go to the dashboard in the upper right hand corner of your site and click on [Support]. Scroll to the bottom of that page. Click on [Still need help?].

Click on [Contact us]. This opens a help window. You need to type in several words to activate [Ask Question]. After doing that scroll down to the bottom and click on [Contact Support].

This opens up [How would you like to contact us?] Three options are given, e-mail, chat or talk to me. NOTE: you need to have a Pro subscription or higher to access live telephone support.

Telephone Support

If you have a Pro subscription or higher, scroll to the bottom of the help window and click on [Let's Talk]. This will open another window with Weebly's telephone number +1 (844) 493-3259) given as Step One and an eight digit code provided as Step Two. Call the telephone number and insert the code.

The technicians are often very busy and you may wait an extended period of time. If you're fortunate enough to get Nate, or someone equally qualified, you will obtain answers to your questions.

~CHAPTER EIGHTEEN~
Editing, Proofreading
And
Miscellaneous Resources

SELF-EDITING, REVISION and PROOFREADING

Editing and proofreading are two methods of revision. They are often used interchangeably, but they differ. To better understand their nature and to avoid confusion, we will examine them separately.

Editing

Editing is a continuous activity. It begins with the planning phase. It continues as ideas are explored and writing has begun. Words are transformed into text. The document continues to be edited until the final draft is completed. Windows Speech Recognition is ideal for speeding up the process.

Editing deals with overall meaning and presentation. The intent is to improve the overall quality of the language and the expression of ideas and to provide clarity and readability. Potential changes are considered that affect the style, point-of-view, and organization of content suitable for the intended audience.

Proofreading

Proofreading focuses on correcting errors in spelling, syntax, grammar, punctuation, formatting, and other language mistakes. Most writers, even with considerable writing experience, admit they have difficulty recognizing structural or grammatical errors. For that reason, careful self-editing, revision, rewriting and proofreading are necessary to spot errors and discover potential changes to improve writing. Proofreading can take much more time than writing the first draft. But it provides the writer with another tool to more closely perfect their work.

Learning Writing Skills

Our reference to the following applications is not to teach writing skills. We will leave those skills to those qualified by education, experience, and temperament. If you seek to improve your style and content, many books and websites are devoted to this.

To produce quality work, it is essential that the writer consider these elements. They are so important that we would be remiss if we did not introduce resources that we have discovered that will assist the writer in addressing them.

These programs will not relieve the writer from the task of thoroughly evaluating their work. They will not replace the writers' judgment in deciding if any changes should be made. However, they provide tools to teach a writer how to develop insight into better writing practices.

Words from a Professional

A book recognized as a classic on how to improve writing is *On Writing Well* by William Zinsser.

The Importance of Improving Your Writing Skills

He captures the art of writing with his experience, warmth and wisdom. This will remind you of some of the important aspects of good writing, and also introduce you to an authoritative resource.

On Writing Well - William Zinsser

Mr. Zinsser was a writer, editor and teacher. He taught writing at Yale, New School and Columbia University Graduate School of Journalism. He wrote 17 books. He knew how to write, how to edit, and how to teach others these skills.

On the jacket of *On Writing Well, The Classic Guide to Writing Nonfiction the 30th Anniversary Edition,* the book is described as:

> It is a book for anybody who wants to learn how to write, whether about people and places, science and technology, business, sports, the arts, or about yourself.

On Writing Well underscores some of the important aspects of good writing.

The Secret of Good Writing

> But the secret of good writing is to strip every sentence to its cleanest components. Every word that serves no function, every long word that could be a short word, every adverb that carries the same meaning that's already in the verb, every passive construction that leaves the reader unsure of who is doing what – these are the thousand and one adulterants that weaken the strength of a sentence. And they usually occur in proportion to education and rank. (Pages 6-7)

And whether it is called self-editing, revision, rewriting, or proofreading, Mr. Zinsser gives us insight into the importance of rewriting as part of the development of better writing skills.

Rewriting

> Rewriting is the essence of writing well: it's where the game is won or lost. That idea is hard to accept. We all have an emotional equity in our first draft; we can't believe that it wasn't born perfect. But the odds are close to 100 percent that it wasn't. Most readers don't initially say what they want to say, or say it as well as they could.
>
> The newly hatched sentence almost always has something wrong with it. It is not clear. It's not logical. It's verbose. It's klunky. It's pretentious. It's boring. It's full of clutter. It's full of clichés. It lacks rhythm. It can be read in several different

ways. It doesn't lead out of the previous sentence. It doesn't... The point is that clear writing is the result of a lot of tinkering. (Pages 83-84)

Hard Work

Writing is hard work. The clear sentence is no accident. Very few sentences come out right the first time, or even the third time. Remember this in moments of despair. If you find that writing is hard, it's because it is hard. (Page 9)

Encouragement

Some additional words of encouragement from Mr. Zinsser are found again in *On Writing Well*. Not everyone will appreciate your work. Do not be discouraged.

> A good editor likes nothing better than a piece of copy he hardly has to touch. A bad editor has a compulsion to tinker, proving with busywork that he hasn't forgotten the minutiae of grammar and usage. He is a literal fellow, catching cracks in the road but not enjoying the scenery. Very often it simply doesn't occur to him that a writer is writing by ear, trying to achieve a particular sound or cadence, or playing with words just for the pleasures of wordplay. One of the bleakest moments for writers is the one when they realize that their editor has missed the point of what they are trying to do. (Page 300)

End of Quotes from *On Writing Well*

To produce quality books, it is essential that the writer consider these fundamentals. We will introduce a number of resources. They will not replace the writer's judgment. However, they will provide information to develop insight into better writing and revising practices.

Some will call attention to potential improvements. Others will provide suggestions to help make decisions. Through continued editing and proofreading, a writer will become more sensitive to structure and grammar.   Mr. Zinseer suggests detailed things to consider when editing. His ideas may seem unduly critical and detailed, but even if you are writing only for your own enjoyment observing them will help you become more attentive and improve your writing style.

Learn How to Track Changes

Save time editing and proofreading documents. Track Changes is an accessory under [Review], which has been part of Microsoft Word, at least since Word 2003. It is also an accessory in OpenOffice and LibreOffice free word processors we discussed earlier. Options are similar. NOTE: Do not learn by activating it for the first time on a long paper.

To review but NOT Track Changes do not click on [Track Changes] but also double-check for [No Markup]. To activate use [Review] and [Track Changes]. Use Simple Markup, All Markup, No Markup or Original. View changes while creating in a Reviewing Pane.

It will make you more proficient in evaluating your thoughts. Learning it will increase your ability to edit and proofread. When activated [Track Changes] records changes made by the user. ~~If a word, phrase, sentence or an entire paragraph is deleted, it marks it with strike-through.~~ If words are added, they are underlined.

When finished, start with the first sentence use [Next]. When moving through a document edits are chosen by [Next] or [Previous].

The user chooses to [Accept] or [Reject] what has been marked. If accepted, words marked for deletion are deleted, words added will be inserted into the text. If the marked changes are rejected, the text remains the same and the marking is removed.

FREE ONLINE APPLICATIONS AND RESOURCES

Other speech recognition applications are available for PCs, either as freestanding applications, or special applications such as Google

Apps. Most notably; Speechnotes, SpeechnotesX - Voice Testing, and Google Docs (Docs.google.com). Access them by opening the Google Chrome browser.

The Google API speech recognition-data base is extensive. With experience, most users can produce good results. If typing is a real problem for shorter projects these can be of help.

Many of these applications also work with Apple MacBooks, making speech recognition easier for those users as well. The chief advantage? They do not require completing a tutorial before using them.

The disadvantage? Limited ability to edit text by voice commands. They do not permit "editing on the fly." If you make a mistake, changes are made manually, not by voice.

For editing, they require the mouse and/or the [Delete] and [Backspace] keys. Because they are reasonably accurate, however, when used to produce smaller documents, with experience, editing can often be minimal.

Slickwrite Online

We are including additional information on this application because for a free application it does a thorough job of evaluating a document. Some writers might conclude that it is too thorough. Nevertheless, it is worth checking out.

Opening this application with Internet Explorer will permit using Windows Speech Recognition. If not using Windows Speech Recognition, you can type or [Paste] text into the application. The results will be the same, it will just take a little longer.

Search for Slickwrite as one word, if not you will be encouraged to buy marking pencils. The name of the site is Slickwrite, not Slick Write. For a complete description of options visit the website. Slickwrite will open with [Clear] and [Copy] at the top and 10 icons on the [Left] margin. Take time to check out the menu items.

Click the [Pencil]. You can begin speaking in the text area or, [Paste] a file into this application. You can continue using Speech Recognition, but only in the [Edit] (pencil) screen.

A checkmark appears on the [Left] margin and also on the top. Pressing either will check the document. You will first see [reading…] then [writing…]. This will place the document in critique mode.

To modify how it evaluates a document check out the [Settings]. A document can be evaluated for numerous characteristics. Continue trying all its features. Determine which elements, and which combinations are most helpful for you. It can also be used as a tool to check elements of grammar and style.

grammark.org.

Another free application is **grammark.org.** We are familiar with Serenity Editor, ProWriterAid and Grammarly, for a free on-line application this one has a lot to offer. The developer freely admits that it does not check for many grammar errors. But it does a decent job of evaluating a manuscript focusing on eight grammar issues.

COMMERCIAL EDITORS

We have consistently presented free applications. Editing, revision, and proofreading are so important we are modifying that practice to recommend three commercial applications for those who wish to evaluate their documents more thoroughly.

Serenity Editor

We have reviewed as many as one hundred websites and dozens of products researching for this tutorial. Not all were free. This one is worth considering. It can be used with the Microsoft Word, WordPad, and other word editors and processors. Because of its thorough evaluation, and its many suggestions, we recommend downloading the 10-day free trial if still available.

Grammarly

Grammarly provides add-on apps for Google and Microsoft Word. Once installed in Google Chrome it will assist in spelling and grammar in Gmail and on websites. We have used their free apps and they do a good job in identifying word spacing, punctuation errors, and grammar. All this for free. They advertise personalizing it for free.*

ProWriterAid

ProWriterAid is another grammar and spelling application. Several articles on the Internet compare it to Grammarly. Evaluators seem evenly divided on which they prefer. It also has add-on apps for Google, Microsoft Word and other popular word processing applications. A no-cost trial period is available.

We did not buy a subscription to Grammarly. We did buy Serenity Editor and ProWriterAid. We are familiar with the free version of Grammarly. We would conclude based on our experience and what we have read that any reader needing a more comprehensive tool should review all three of these. Any one of them will accomplish that. Individual preferences do matter. Check them out and their prices as well.

FREE INTERNET RESOURCES

There are hundreds of sites that present credible information that will benefit anyone seeking to improve their writing skills. We are including a few that we have found helpful which in some cases provide a virtual encyclopedia of resources. Our apology to those we might have missed.

---

* Grammarly terms. By signing up you agree to the Terms and Conditions and Privacy Policy. You also agree to receive product-related emails from Grammarly, which you can unsubscribe from at any time.

Tech Tools for Writers

This site is well designed and hosted by Corina Koch MacLeod. It is

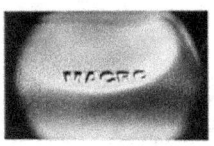

worth visiting for all its content. Well designed, authored and interesting. For Microsoft 2010 and later Word users, visit Self-Editing Tools and Macros.

Archive Publications http://www.archivepub.co.uk

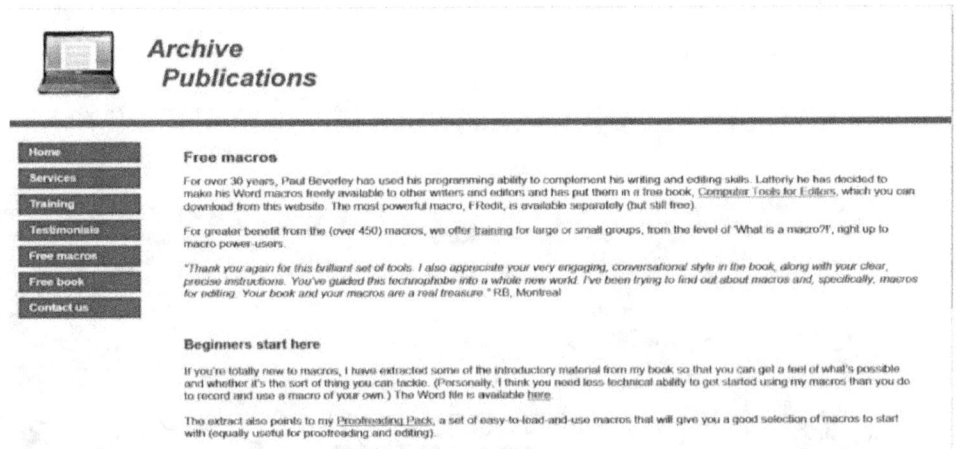

The above site is yet another of several referred to by Corina. This is the site of Paul Beverly, who provides advanced Word Macros to further refine proofreading. He provides some powerful editing tools.

Beyond Paper Editing

Another site introduced by Corina. More excellent articles. Choose topics of interest. Many useful suggestions.

Beyond Paper Editing

Another site introduced by Corina. More excellent articles. Choose topics of interest. Many useful suggestions.

GrammarBook.com

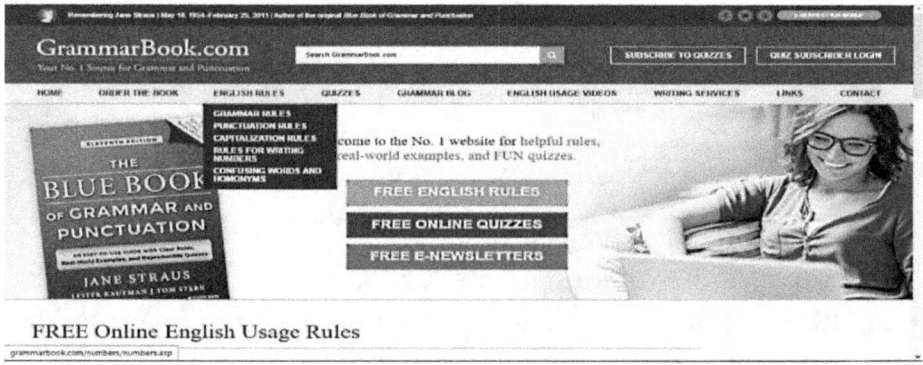

GrammarBook.com introduces the reader to the *Blue Book of Grammar and Punctuation*. It is also available in book form. It has numerous topics and Online Quizzes. These show numerous examples of usage. This is a quick check for a fundamental review of grammar.

Now in its 8th Edition. The 7th edition is available in PDF form at: http://www.e-reading.club/bookreader.php/134334/The_Blue_Book_of_Grammar_and_Punctuation.pdf

Virustotal

Virustotal.com was mentioned earlier. It is a free service that analyzes suspicious files and URLs on more than fifty sites. Available online and as a download. Search by File, URL or Search. Checks for viruses, worms, Trojans and malware. A good pre-test of a new application

The Chicago Manual of Style

http://www.chicagomanualofstyle.org/tools_citationguide.html
A long-time standard. Now online. Search for free back issues.

WikiHow to Do Anything…

Here one can search for and find information on how to do almost anything. This site, while having information on editing and proofreading, also has information on how to do many things. For an example, those who have an interest in videos, will find an article on How to Make a YouTube Video. We are not including this topic in this tutorial.

https://owl.english.purdue.edu/owl/resource/717/07/

The Purdue Online Writing Lab (OWL)
https://owl.english.purdue.edu

A site comparable to the UNC site below. Review this and the following site for ideas and examples. .

The Writing Center at the University of North Carolina

http://writingcenter.unc.edu/handouts/

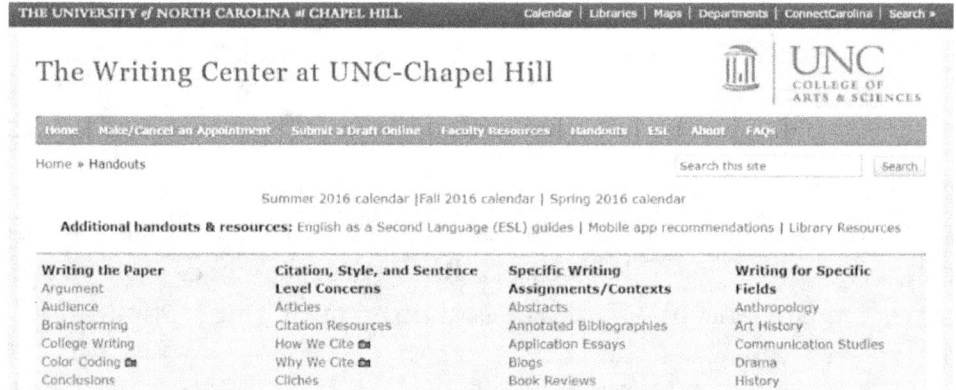

Citing Sources? University of North Carolina Libraries

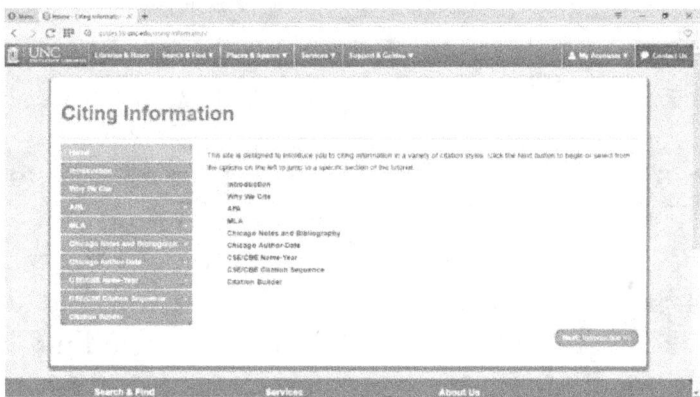

Citing sources is always a headache when doing research or quoting a large number of sources. Several websites make this easier. We have not found any better than the University of North Carolina Libraries.

It covers all the important authorities in a well-organized format. It also includes an introduction to the purpose of citation and what needs to be cited. Easy to find at http://guides.lib.unc.edu/citing-information/, or by searching for: Home – Citing Information – LibGuides at the University of North Carolina.

The Book Designer
http://www.the-bookdesigner.com

Joel Friedlander was a frequent contributor to CreateSpace, now Kindle Direct Publishing He is a reliable source for information on designing books. We do not know if he continues to be a resource for KDP.

Pat McNees ~ Writers and Editors

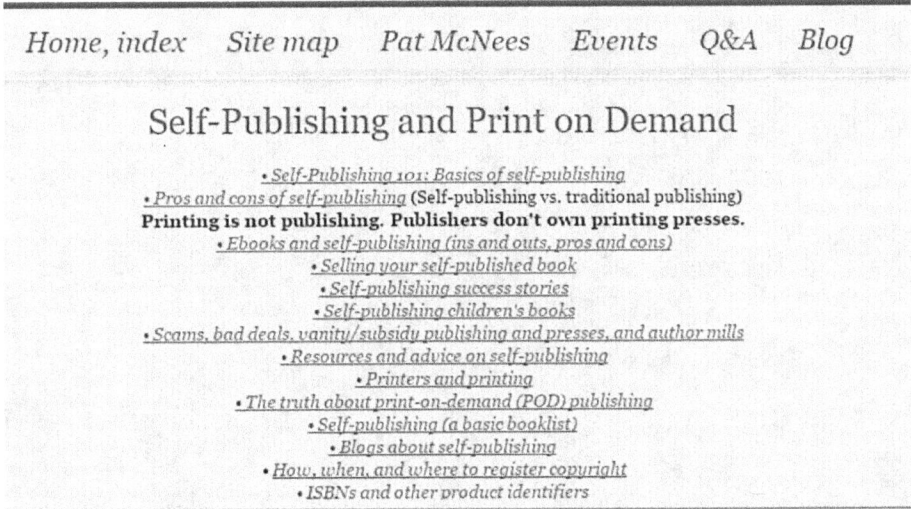

This website is an encyclopedia of topics of interest to writers, authors, editors and self-publishers. It covers the extensive field of writing and associated endeavors. From Acquiring, Selling and Swapping Books, through Agents and Book Proposals, Blogs, Book covers, Copyright, Fact-checking sites, Ebook Basics, Fiction Writing, Ghostwriting, Self-Publishing and Print on Demand (POD). Well-Designed Author's Websites, Writing White Papers and more.

~APPENDIX~

ALTERNATE FREE SPEECH RECOGNITION APPS

Speech recognition has come into its own, especially with Smartphones. Many people create text messages by dictating to their phone. They no longer key them in except to correct errors. They also dictate the contents of e-mails and transmit them without having to [Cut] and [Paste]. Why? Because it is easier than typing. Accuracy is sometimes a problem (but not always) and even when it is, it is less frustrating to re-dictate just a portion of the message, and/or if necessary, make a few corrections manually.

Microsoft Windows Speech Recognition is not the only free speech recognition application for PCs. Google, through its extensive search engine has assembled a huge database. Developers use this with their speech recognition applications to compose text messages without first creating a user's profile.

Speechnotes

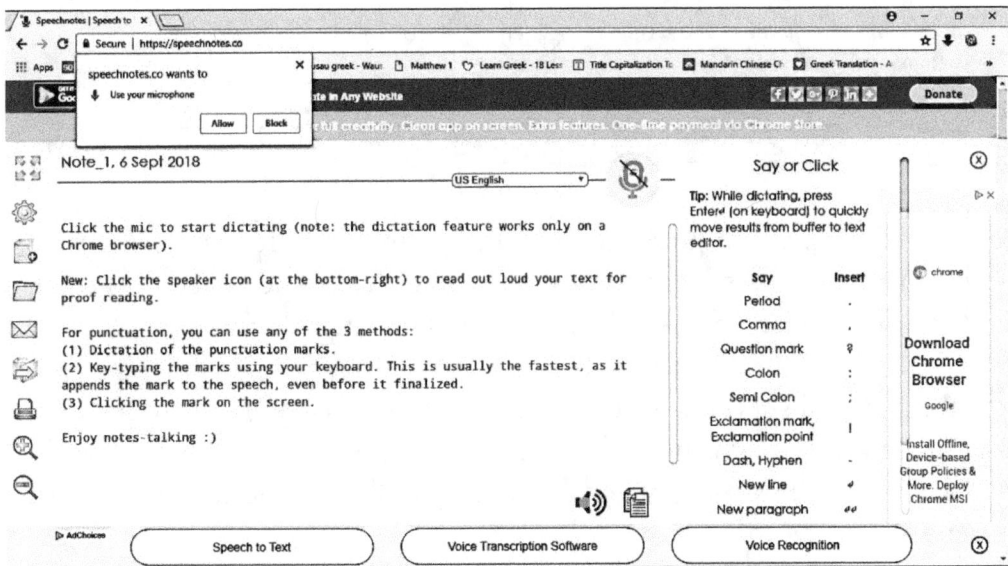

This above image shows how Speechnotes appears when it is first opened. It is not necessary to download this application. Search for and [Open] Speechnotes in the Google Chrome Browser. It is not necessary to complete any tutorials to use this application. The first screen will request the use of your microphone [Allow]. Set the cursor on the page then click on the microphone in the upper [Right] hand corner and begin composing.

This does not permit correction "on the fly." Watch for errors when composing because manual corrections need to be made during creation and editing.

Example Speechnotes

Because it does not require creating a user profile before use, it can be used "out of the box." Not quite the "Eureka" experience. You still need to consciously speak clearly, but it is getting closer.

For many it will serve as an easy way to create notes. For others who create numerous and longer documents it will serve as an incentive to try Microsoft Windows Speech Recognition to experience the benefit of making corrections by voice.

The advantage, no need to create a user's profile. The disadvantage, errors created by voice cannot be immediately be corrected by voice. They must be corrected manually. This application is only available on Google Chrome. It also works with Apple MacBook and Android devices. Data can be transferred between non-Microsoft devices and Microsoft operating systems by email.

Google Docs

Google Chrome also has an online word processor called Google Docs. It is a word processor and has those features one expects to see in a word processor.

This is also accessed by googling Google Docs. It opens as a word processing application in the Windows version. We are showing an image of its microphones below. Its appearance can be better understood by opening the application, reading the instructions from Google, and creating text.

The speech recognition function is first activated by opening [Add-ons]. Select (speech recognition) there. Next, enter [Tools] and select (voice typing).

A black and white microphone icon will appear on the [Left]. It can be moved if the user finds it more convenient in another location.

When activated the microphone image changes to a microphone surrounded by a red circle. When dictating, circles expand out beyond the initial circle, to show that it is processing.

This is a word processor and it has those functions associated with a word processors. Because Google Docs is a word processor it has many features not shared by Speechnotes, but like Speechnotes it does not permit editing by voice recognition.

If the reader experiments with either of these, and learns to efficiently make corrections manually, either of them will perform a decent job.

10 TOP TEN REVIEWS – SPEECH RECOGNITION TEST

Following is a copy of the test referred to earlier in this tutorial. It was the test appeared on 10 TopTen Reviews. (Sometimes simply called Top Ten Reviews.) It is an informative website on many subjects of interest to users of computers and electronic fixtures.

We first became aware of it in June of 2012. The test is reproduced with their permission. All participants received identical paragraphs containing 125 words and 15 punctuation marks. Any error in composing words or punctuation counts.

Recently the test was still available on their website. In any event we received permission to include it in this tutorial.

> This text was created as a trial of the voice recognition software we tested for this review. The same reviewer read this text in the dictation mode of each program. By using the same text and the same voice profile, we can get a pretty good idea of how accurately each program translates speech, allowing us to compare them. Any errors in dictation will be in bold, so you can easily see where the program made the mistakes. The number of errors will be counted (including punctuation errors) and combined to give an accuracy score for each program. And to create a real challenge, we'll include a few humdinger colloquialisms, by golly. We'll see if these groovy programs can jive with less stuffy lingo. Savvy?

The participants were texted twice. Their test results were as follows: The best performer had 9 errors producing 98% accuracy; the second, using the same paragraph, had 17 errors with 93% accuracy.

The third tested out with 19 errors; 92% accuracy; and the, last 34 errors, for an accuracy rating of 86%. As indicated previously, we first completed the test in June of 2012 using Microsoft Word 2003, with 4 errors. We also retested twice in July of 2014 using Windows 7/WordPad first with 4 errors. The second time, because of careless reading, we had 6 errors. We include this for the encouragement of the reader. The point is not whether you score better, but rather to take the test now and again in 3 or 6 months so you can judge your own progress.

PROFILE BACKUP AND RESTORE

When we first began writing two User Profile Backup and Restore Applications were available on the Internet. SpProfileMgr.exe and SRProfile.exe.

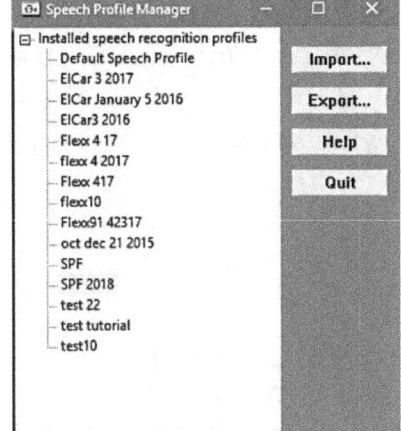

Shown is SpProfileMgr.exe. If you search for this information you will find reference to several sites. Much of the information on this topic however is outdated and you will get to a 404 page, which means the link no longer works. In part this is because SRProfile.exe. is no longer available.

On your USB drive or in your [Music] or [Video] Folder create a file [Speech Profile]. Download this from a genuine Microsoft site. Search for Microsoft Speech Recognition Backup and Restore. The Internet is constantly changing. To give a specific website address might be misleading.

When you open the Manager it will want to store this information on your C drive under the [User] file. Change it to whatever your USB drive letter is (A, etc) and add/ Speech Profile Manager. [Save] both files.

When you open it, SpProfileMger will appear like the image above. To use follow these steps: 1. Open [Help]. After using you must use the microphone wizard for the imported profile. 2. Second, locate your User's Profile in Windows Speech Recognition. Use the following sequence: Control Panel, Ease of Access, Speech

Recognition, Advanced Speech Options.

3. Under Speech Properties to the left of [Delete] is a window which scrolls using the ∧ and ∨ arrows. Scroll to see what speech profiles, it contains. If it only contains the Default Speech Profile you can use that as an example to see how the application works.

4. If only [Default Speech Profile] highlight it. If there are others, you will need to determine which is the best one to duplicate. Highlight it. Use [Export] which will request a file location and a name. 5. You can use your name the month and year (Bubba320.spf) and the last three letters as shown (copy spf). [Save]. Check which is [Saved] by again using [Export] to view the directory.

Already Using Windows Speech Recognition?

If already using Windows Speech Recognition use the same procedure to select your current User's Profile and [Save] to transfer to another computer. Using the USB drive open the application and use [Import] to transfer it to your User's Profile on the new computer. Use the same USB drive on that computer to make the transfer.

Sometimes stubborn extraneous characters or words show up in User's Profiles. You may wish to create a new User's Profile. After you gain experience you will create a better User's Profile. Using the application save it for future reference.

We did an extensive search for WSRProfile.exe including www.OldApps.com but could not find it. Use the current one instead.

OPTIMIZATION UTILITIES

Even if you have good speech habits and a good microphone, speech recognition requires a solid connection between the microphone and a responsive computer. If the connection is compromised, the computer will not function properly, Windows Speech Recognition may perform well but not efficiently.

Optimization includes improving performance by deleting programs never used, limiting how many programs run at startup, defragmenting the hard disk, cleaning up the hard drive, running fewer programs and turning off visual effects.

It can also be improved by restarting your PC regularly. This helps conserve memory and closes all software and services that might have been running in the background. You can improve capacity by adding more memory, but that probably is not necessary. An important rule is to always be on guard for viruses and spyware.

Go on the Internet and search for "Optimize Windows for better performance." We would provide a link, but as we have suggested, links frequently change. This is a Microsoft article and it will get you started. If your computer is running slow run fewer applications at a time. Several applications already on your computer can help.

Already on Your Computer

1. Microsoft Performance Troubleshooter. 2. Microsoft Security Essential, 3. Disk Cleanup and 4. Disk Defragmenter. Optimization is also available through anti-virus programs.

QUICK GUIDES

Quick Guide - Speech Recognition Module

[Show Speech Options] can be opened with that command or a [Right] click on the Speech Recognition Module in all four operating systems.

On: Sleep: Off: 1, 2, and 3. The first three items are the same for all operating systems Experiment to see which works best for you.

1	On: Listen to everything I say
2	Sleep: Listen only for "start listening"
3	Off: Do not listen to anything I say
4	Open Speech Reference Card
5	Start Speech Tutorial
6	Help
7	Options ▶
8	Configuration ▶
9	Open the Speech Dictionary
10	Dictation Topic ▶
11	Help improve Speech Recognition...
12	About Windows Speech Recognition
13	Open Speech Recognition
14	Exit

Key:
A Vista and Windows 7
B Windows 8 And Windows 10

4. A. [Open Speech Reference Card] Open after [Show Speech Options] and [Left] clicking on [Open Speech Reference Card].

Opens the [Windows Help and Support] Common commands in Speech Recognition on the Vista and Windows 7 operating systems..

4. B. In Windows 8 and Windows 10 goes to the Internet.

5. A. [Start Speech Tutorial] Opens interactive speech tutorial on the operating system.

5. B   Windows 8 and Windows 10 goes to the Internet.

6. A. [Help] Opens [Window Help and Support] What can I do with Speech Recognition? On the Vista and Windows 7 operating system.

6. B. In Windows 8 and Windows 10 goes to the Internet.

7. A & B [Options] We are interested only in [Enable dictation scratchpad] which should be checked in all four operating systems.

8. A & B (Configuration)[Speech Recognition Control Panel]. Easiest way for users of Vista and Windows 7 to access the [Configure your Speech Recognition experience].

9. A & B [Open the Speech Dictionary] will open with simply [Open Speech Dictionary] in all four operating systems

10. – 12 Skip.

13. A & B [Open Speech Recognition] returns to [Listening] Speech Recognition Module

14. Good-bye Speech Recognition

TABLE 1 COLUMN A and B

Table 1 Column A

Command	Action	Option
[Start][Control Panel][Ease of Access][Speech Recognition]	To Access Application Create Shortcut	Complete all Microsoft Tutorials
[Start Listening] [What Can I Say?][Show Speech Options]	Open Menu Message Board	Easy Access to Help
[Open/Start] Word-Pad, Word, Excel, etc. [Close that]	Opens/closes Application or Program	{V} [File] [Press][Alt] (f)
[Menu] (New) (Open)(Save/Save as)(Print)(Quick/ Preview)(Page Setup)(Exit)	Alternative [Application] Shows Files Under Menu. Items	{V} [File] Instead of [Menu] and [Application] [Press][Alt](f)
[Show Numbers] [Switch to]	Numbers Menu Items Change Location	Alternative to File Name Location
[Mouse Grid]	Zeros in on Target	Isolates Specific Area of Window
[New Line/ New Paragraph] [Enter][Enter]	Down 1 Line Down 2 Down 1/2	Alternate Command [Enter]
Say Word not [Command]	Produces Word Not Action	[Spell-it] [Say Wrong Word, [Select] and [Correct]
Say a Word not [Number]	Produces the Word (One, Two etc. Not #)	[Spell-it] [Start Spelling]
[Numeral] – Get Number not Word	Produces Numeral not Word	[Press] Number Key

Table 1 Column B

Command	Action	Option
[Press](Shift Key) (Individual Key) (Letters, Symbols or Numbers)	Duplicates Keyboard Entry	Numerous Secondary Commands
[Press] [Home] [End] [Alt][Ctrl] *Spoken Keystrokes:*	Up/Down, Keys Margins	One Unit {V}[Press] Command not Needed
[Go](Up/ Down) (*Line*) [Scroll] (Up /Down) (*Page*)	Navigation Up/Down By Line or Page	Increased Navigation

Commands /Sub-Commands

Command	Action	Option
[Delete] [Delete That]	(Word) (Next/Last/ Previous # of Units)	(Undo That)
[Correct] [Correct That]	(Word) (Next/Last/ Previous # of Units)	(Spell-it) (Start Spelling)
[Select] [Select That] [Unselect That]	(Word) (Next/Last/ Previous # of Units) (Word…Word)	(Unselect That)(Clear) (Arrow Keys)
[Go To] [Move To]	(Word) (Beginning of/End of)	(Word) (Sentence) (Paragraph)
[Go] [Move]	(Before/After) (Forward/ Back)	(Characters) (Word) (Sentence) (Paragraph)
Take Second Series Speech Recognition Voice Training	Train Your Computer	Further Configure Your Computer

©ElCar Publishing August 2014

Experiment with All Commands!

TABLE 2 COLUMN A and B

Table 2 Column A			Table 2 Column B		
Command	Detail	Misc	Other FREE Writer's Tool Kit Items		
Review Quick-Guides	Copies of Quick-Guides in Appendix	Learn how Practice, Practice,	Speech Recognition Macros	Customize WSR Commands	Download Templates From Net
Microsoft WordPad/Word Formatting	[File][Home] [View] [Keys] Shortcuts	[Press][Alt] (F)(H)(V) Shortcuts	Navigation [Switch] to [Desktop]	[Switch Applications]	From Desktop to Applications
[Page Setup] [Margins] [Save][Print]	[File] (Sub – Commands)	Location Varies with Application	Create Tables/ Convert Images	Appearance/ Publication	Presentation of Data
Zoom - Ruler Word Wrap	[View] Set Ruler and Word Wrap	Ruler Formats Text to Screen	PDF Editors PDF Viewers Ultrafilesearch	Convert Files and Images Search	Create Image Produce Text Find Files
Finish WordPad with OpenOffice	Speech Recognition WordPad	[Paste] Format in OpenOffice	Paint.NET	Image Editors Snipping Tool	Convert Image for Document
Lines Paragraphs Alignment	[Home] Spacing Left, Right, Justify	[Press] [Ctrl] [L] [R] [J] [E/Center]	OCR Scrivener yWriter	Recovery Novels and Projects	Digital Text For Writers and Research
Expand Collapse Ribbon	[Home] Increase Text Area	Increase/ Decrease Menu Items	Text-to-Speech Sound Editors	Free and Commercial Applications	TypeIt ReadIt 3 Commercial Applications
[Text] [Font] [Text Color]	[Home] Size Color of fonts Background	Text/Font Term Varies by App	MultiPurpose Caliibre	Library Mgr. e-books	Novelists Detailed Compositions
Bold](B) Underline](U) [Italicize] (I)	Change Appearance of Font	[Press] [Ctrl] (B) (U) (I) Repeat	Self-Motivated Author	Self-Publishing I Ought to Write a Book	Paperback KDP- Smash-words e-Books
[Caps/No Cap/ Lower Case Headings	Caps No Caps Modified Headings	[Press] [Ctrl] (E)(L)(R)(J)	Create Your Own Website	Free Website and Domain	Weebly and Others
[Insert] Picture/ Draw	WordPad Check out Draw	[Word] [Insert] Application	Self-editing Revision and Proofreading	Free Online Resources Commercial	Slickwrite Hemingway Grammarly
[Copy][Paste] Vs [Cut] [Paste]	Note Page # [Copy][Paste] Return [Cut]	Copy data Move/ Paste Return/Delete	Commercial Editors	Serenity Editor Grammarly	For the Serious Prolific Writer
[Press][Ctrl] (f) (h)	Find and Replace	Search/Find/ Replace	Free Internet Resources Viristotal	Tech Tools And Otherss File check	Resources on Line
Enable Dictation Scratchpad	Extend Use of Speech Recognition	Other Apps Other than Microsoft	Quick-Guides Tables 1 & 2 Other Guides	Miscellaneous Helps Wrap up	Additional Information on Subjects

ElCar Publishing August 2018

Experiment with [Show Numbers] and [Mouse Grid] on Internet!

NATO ALPHABET SIGNS & SYMBOLS

NATO ALPHABET ~ SIGNS ~ SYMBOLS

NATO Alphabet / Letter – Code

A as in ALFA
B – BRAVO
C – CHARLIE
D – DELTA
E – ECHO
F – FOXTROT
G – GOLF
H – HOTEL
I – INDIA
J – JULIETT
K – KILO
L – LIMA
M – MIKE
N – NOVEMBER
O – OSCAR
P – PAPA
Q – QUEBEC
R – ROMEO
S – SIERRA
T – TANGO
U – UNIFORM
V – VICTOR
W – WHISKEY
X – XRAY
Y – YANKEE
Z – ZULU

Common Punctuation Marks & Characters.

(.) Period; Dot; Full Stop; Decimal Point
(,) Comma
(:) Colon
(;) Semicolon
(?) Question mark
(') Apostrophe
(!) Exclamation Mark; Exclamation Point
(¶) Paragraph Sign
(+) Plus Sign
(-) Hyphen; Minus Sign; Dash
(=) Equal Sign
(×) Multiplication Sign
(÷) Division Sign

Frequently Used Punctuation Marks & Characters

(") Open/Close Double Quotes
(') Open/Close Single Quote
(*) Asterisk
(@) At Sign
(_) Underscore
(&) Ampersand, And Sign
(/) Forward Slash
(\ ) Backslash
(#) Number Sign
(   ) Open/Close Parentheses
[   ] Open/Close Brackets
{   } Open/Close Brace, Open Curly Bracket
(°) Degree Sign
(§) Section Sign
(>) Greater Than Sign: Open Angle Bracket
(<) Less than Sign: Close Angle Bracket
($) Dollar Sign
(¢) Cent Sign
(£) Pound Sign
(¥) Yen (Japan) Yuan (China)
(¼) One Quarter Sign
(½) One Half Sign
(¾) Three Quarter Sign
(©) Copyright Sign
(®) Registered Sign, Reg. Trademark Sign
(™) Trademark Sign
(~) Tilde (Common in Ebooks)

Less Common Punctuation Marks & Characters

(–) En Dash
(—) Em Dash, Double Dash
(…) Ellipsis; Dot dot dot
(|) Vertical Bar
(//) Double Slash
(`) Back Quote (Bottom Tilde Key)
(«) Open Angle Quote
(») Close Angle Quote

Elear Publishing March 2017

ALTERNATE COMMANDS

Alternate Commands Using [Press] [Alt]/[Ctrl]

WordPad and Word 2003 - {W} if Other

Menu Commands [Press] [Alt]

[Press][Alt] [f] = File/Application

[Press][Alt] [h] = Home {W} = Help

[Press][Alt] [v] = View {W} = View

Format Commands [Press] [CTRL] [ ]

[Press][CTRL] [a] = Selects entire manuscript

[Press][CTRL] [b] = Bold (must first select words to change.)

[Press][CTRL] [i] = Italics (must first select words to change.)

[Press][CTRL] [u] = Underline (must first select words to change.)

[Press][CTRL] [d] {W} = Font

Bitmap Image

[Press][CTRL] [d] = *Bitmap Image in Document - Paint.* This will open an application showing a box.

If you do not add anything in the box, it will appear as an open space between the previous text line and one that follows this command. To delete it, left mouse click in the open area. The borders will appear. You can then delete it.

But you can also add pictures, draw with the Mouse in the box, and several other options. Review this unique feature and experiment with the features to add variety to your documents. Not part of {W}.

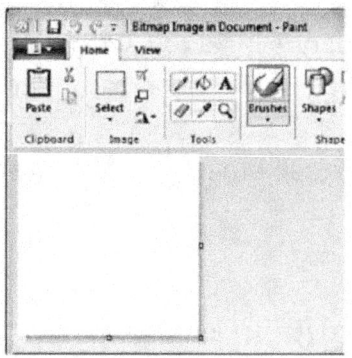

TEN MORE

[Press] [CTRL] [f] = Find

[Press] [CTRL] [h] = Replace (works to find/replace words)

[Press][CTRL] [n] = New

[Press] [CTRL] [o] = Open

[Press][CTRL] [p] = Print

[Press][CTRL] [r] = Right alignment

[Press][CTRL] [l] = Left alignment

[Press][CTRL] [e] = Center alignment

[Press][CTRL] [v] = Paste

[Press][CTRL] [z] = Delete

© ElCar Publishing July 2014

MORE ALTERNATE KEY COMMANDS

[Press]/ [Alt] [F Keys] [Ctrl] or [Shift]

The Image from Wikipedia

These key [Commands] do not work in every application. Experiment to see which works with the application you are using. For voice commands preface with [Press]. If using the commands manually omit [Press]. These came from various sources.

To reverse change = Repeat the [Command].

Emphasizing Text

[Bold] = [Press] [Ctrl] (B) Repeat to Unbold
[Italicize] = [Press] [Ctrl] (I)
[Underline] = [Press] [Ctrl] (U)

Margins

[Right]   [Press] [Ctrl] (R)
[Center]   [Press] [Ctrl] (E)
[Left]   [Press] [Ctrl] (L)
[Justify] [Press] [Ctrl] (J)

Utility

[Press] [Ctrl] (N) (New blank document)
[Press] [Ctrl] (O) (Open a file)
[Insert] (Picture/Paint Drawing)
[Insert] (Date and Time/Object)
[Press] [Alt] (F) (Opens file menu options)
[Press] [Alt] (Tab) (Switch between open programs)

[Press] [Alt] + (Enter) (Open properties for selected item - file, folder, shortcut, etc.)

[Press] [F1]   (Universal Help)
[Press] [Ctrl] (A) (Select all text)
[Press] [Ctrl] (C) (Copy)
[Press] [Ctrl] (K) (Insert hyperlink)
[Press] [Ctrl] (P) (Print current page or document)
[Press] [Ctrl] (V) (Paste)
[Press] [Ctrl] (S) (Saves document or other file)
[Press] [Ctrl] (Esc) (Opens the start menu)
[Press] [Ctrl] (End) (Goes to end of the document)
[Press] [Ctrl] (Home) (Goes to beginning of document)

[Windows Key] - Wikipedia

For [Commands] following the [Windows], [Command]. See article on Wikipedia website, which shows over 50 ways how the [Windows key] and various (Subcommands) respond with Microsoft Operating Systems from Windows 95 to Windows 8.1 and Microsoft Office. March 2017

Screen Shot from Wikipedia Article on Windows key

≡Win + S activates the Search Everywhere charm, opening a sidebar at the side of the screen.
≡Win + U activates the Ease of Access Center control panel applet
≡Win + V cycles through notifications

ElCar Publishing Website

QUICK GUIDES
http://www.elcarpublishing.com

Contact us with your questions, or comments, on our Home page. Ask for free copies of our Quick-Guides, suitable for printing on card stock.   Copyright © 2018 ElCar Publishing, LLC. El Mirage, AZ December 2018.

~Notes~

~Notes~

~Notes~

~Notes~

www.ingramcontent.com/pod-product-compliance
Lightning Source LLC
Chambersburg PA
CBHW081426220526
45466CB00008B/2289